Scoundrels

*Defining Corruption Through Tales of
Political Intrigue in Rhode Island*

PAUL F. CARANCI & THOMAS BLACKE

Scoundrels:
Defining Corruption Through Tales of Political Intrigue in Rhode Island
By
Paul F. Caranci
& Thomas Blacke

Scoundrels: Corruption and Politics in Rhode Island
Copyright © 2016 Paul F. Caranci. Produced and printed by Stillwater River Publications. All rights reserved. Written and produced in the United States of America. This book may not be reproduced or sold in any form without the expressed, written permission of the authors and publisher.
Visit our website at **www.StillwaterPress.com** for more information.
First Stillwater River Publications Edition
ISBN-10: 0-692-60192-9
ISBN-13: 978-069260192-1

Library of Congress Control Number: 2015960194

Publisher's Cataloging-In-Publication Data
(Prepared by The Donohue Group, Inc.)

Names: Caranci, Paul F. | Blacke, Thomas.
Title: Scoundrels : defining corruption through tales of
    political intrigue in Rhode Island / Paul F. Caranci &
    Thomas Blacke.
Description: First Stillwater River Publications edition. |
    Glocester, RI, USA : Stillwater River Publications,
    [2016] | Includes bibliographical references.
Identifiers: LCCN 2015960194 | ISBN 0-692-60192-9 | ISBN
    978-0-692-60192-1
Subjects: LCSH: Political corruption--Rhode Island. | Pub-
    lic administration--Moral and ethical aspects--Rhode Is-
    land. | Rhode Island--Politics and government.
Classification: LCC JF1081 .C37 2016 F85 | DDC
    364.132309745--dc23

1 2 3 4 5 6 7 8 9 10
Written by Paul F. Caranci & Thomas Blacke
Cover design by Dawn M. Porter.
Published by Stillwater River Publications, Glocester, RI, USA.

DEDICATION

This book is dedicated to all those elected and appointed public officials who have had the courage to expose corruption only to find that honesty and integrity are not without cost.

CONTENTS

ACKNOWLEDGMENTS

We would like to acknowledge with gratitude the efforts of many people that made this book possible. These include Tracey Croce from the Office of the RI Secretary of State and Ms. Kathleen Needham of *The Woonsocket Call* for providing many of the photographs that appear in the book, Tom Evans, the State Librarian for his research assistance, and to the countless people throughout Rhode Island and the United States that stand-up against government and political corruption.

INTRODUCTION

In the year 2004 the Federal Bureau of Investigation began to seek indictments resulting from a lengthy investigation of Rhode Island officials known as Operation Dollar Bill. The ongoing investigation into corruption at the Rhode Island State House resulted in the indictment, resignation and imprisonment of one powerful state senator, the resignation of a Senate President, and the indictment, guilty plea and imprisonment of one former state representative who chaired the powerful House Committee on Corporations. The investigation also touched the business community where it resulted in the indictment, trial, guilty verdict and imprisonment of two high level employees of the Roger Williams Medical Center, an affiliate of the Roger Williams Hospital and subsequently, the dismissal of four long-time and high-level employees of Blue Cross/Blue Shield of RI. To avoid indictment, the companies themselves accepted millions of dollars in fines and agreed to cooperate with all aspects of the federal investigation.

Operation Dollar Bill is just one in a string of Rhode Island corruption scandals that have led to the imprisonment of governors, legislators, mayors, town administrators, council members and a host of other political operatives.

Rhode Island is a small state geographically. With a population of just over one million people, it is probable that most residents have a relationship with one of their elected officials, or at least know someone that does. It is a state in which political relationships have been described as incestuous, and that may be more true than not. Perhaps it is this closeness that tends to lead people in Rhode Island to believe that theirs is the most corrupt state in the union. Leslie Alan Horvitz, in *"Corruption Reaches Fork in the Rhode – Political Corruption in Rhode Island,"* noted, "Rhode Island may not be the most corrupt state in the country, but the electorate can be forgiven for thinking it is."[1] Horvitz continues, after a round of scandals in 1993, some crusaders called "for an entire overhaul of the government." What they got was the RI Ethics Commission. In a final observation Horvitz noted, "If reform can succeed in Rhode Island, it can succeed anywhere."

Certainly criticism of the ethics of Rhode Island elected officials may have never been more persistent, and while the Ethics Commission was deigned to alleviate political corruption, the organization's objective has not even approached mission accomplished status as political corruption continues to flourish in this small state nearly unabated.

This book defines political corruption and uses Rhode Island stories to provide examples of the types of political corruption identified. It is impossible to assess Rhode Island's corruption, or at least to fully grasp its impact on government and society as a whole, without first having at least a cursory discussion of what corruption is and how it is measured.

It is believed that political corruption is as old as government itself. One corruption scholar argues that it may be as old as organized human life! *The Arthashastra*, a 2400-year old text about the government of India, contains a writing authored by Kautilya, an advisor to India's

Maurya Empire founder Chadragupta Maurya. In it, Kautilya discusses how corruption becomes an inevitable component of the Kings maritime routes frequented by the importers of goods. His detailed description provides a meticulous explanation of the corruption that existed in the ancient world. He writes, in part, "...Just as it is impossible not to taste honey or poison that one may find at the tip of one's tongue, so it is impossible for a government servant not to eat up at least a bit of the King's revenue.... And there are about forty ways of embezzlement by the government servant." India did not hold the monopoly on corrupt activities however. Rome, Greece, China and other government structures were besieged equally by the corrosive impact of corruption.

Government corruption has a denigrating effect on society. It clearly increases the cost of government and slows government response to an issue. It hampers economic development and growth, has a negative impact on tax rates and the rate of return on investments, undermines democracy and the civil society and increases the overall cynicism toward government, politics and public servants.

Despite its timeless nature and devastating impact on society, political corruption remains an elusive term that is very difficult to define. Describing political corruption as a cross-systematic, a cross-temporal and a cross cultural phenomenon, noted sociologist Robert Neild contends that corruption exists in all countries, at all times and under every form of government and may be considered the norm for most of human history. A cynical view for sure, but Neild's contention might be regarded as prescient by observers of the American political system. Yet, political corruption exists at so many levels simultaneously, that academic definition remains elusive. The latter half of the 20th century marked the first time that any serious attempts were made to study political corruption on an academic level. Sociologists, political scientists and economists each took a stab at defining political corruption beginning as early as the 1950s. Despite over 60 years of effort, there is not even an academic consensus on the effects of political corruption. While moralists focus on the societal, economic and political scourge of corruption, revisionists cry out for a more objective study of corruption arguing that corruption need not be considered harmful, but rather an "inevitable and necessary part of the adjustment process. Nathaniel Leff even argued that bureaucratic corruption could, in some instances, actually promote efficiency," according to a study written by Mark Jorgensen Farrales for the University of California, San Diego. Such attempts to justify political corruption will find no sympathy in this book. In fact, any fool-hardy attempt to rationalize this inexcusable behavior is rejected out of hand. Rather, greater emphasis will be placed on efforts to try to define political corruption so as to make it understandable, not justifiable, to the reader.

Current academic studies focus on an emerging theory offered by the functionalists. They view political corruption, not as a structural phenomenon or a necessary part of modernization, but rather as an individual choice – carefully calculated decisions intended to confer the greatest benefit possible to the perpetrator of the corrupt act. This view is more in line with modern thinking and represents a greater understanding of political corruption and its impact on society. Yet, not all political corruption is considered illegal. Put another way, a political act doesn't need to be a direct violation of the law to be considered corrupt so long as the act has the same corrosive effects on society as do the illegal acts of political corruption. Unethical or immoral behavior may not constitute a direct violation of any law or ordinance, but may have a deleterious effect on society none-the-less. In that sense, an understanding of political corruption may be defined more by the societal impact of the act than by a standard of law.

The difficulty in defining political corruption, however, does not impede the ability to describe the elemental foundation of the practice. Like sin itself, political corruption can be both active and passive, and each of these corruption types can be exhibited in three categories; traditional, circumstantial and situational.

Active political corruption occurs when a person uses his or her position to participate in the commission of a criminal, unethical or immoral act and is the type of corruption most often prosecuted by law enforcement agencies and displayed in newspaper headlines. Cases of active political corruption will often dominate news media stories and is therefore often presumed to be the only type of political corruption that exists. *Traditional active political corruption* will manifest itself through the extortion demands of a public official or the acceptance of a bribe by a public official.

Active circumstantial political corruption ensues when a public official takes advantage of current circumstances to enrich him or herself. In this case there is both a direct personal benefit to the official and an adverse impact to the public being served.

Active situational political corruption arises when a public official, because of his or her position, is presented with a situation that serves either the public good or the good of an individual and makes a choice to serve the individual needs. There may be no direct benefit to the public official other than performing a favor for another in the hope of remaining in that person's good graces for future consideration.

Passive political corruption occurs when there is awareness by a public official that another official, perhaps a colleague, is committing a criminal, unethical and/or immoral act but allows the activity to continue unabated. In this sense, the official violates his or her fiduciary responsibility to the people he or she is elected to serve and contributes to, perhaps even actually fosters, the deleterious effects of the other person's corrupt acts by allowing those acts to continue.

As before, *passive traditional political corruption* involves a public official's knowledge of another official's acts of bribery and or extortion without taking any steps to stop or expose it.

Passive circumstantial political corruption occurs when a public official knows that another official is taking advantage of current circumstances to directly benefit from an illegal, immoral or unethical act but chooses to remain silent allowing the action to continue unabated.

Finally, *passive situational political corruption* takes place when a public official refuses to interfere in an action despite having knowledge that another official is using a situation to prevent someone entitled to a certain governmental action from receiving that benefit. Generally there is no immediate benefit for the public official who is aware of the corrupt act taking place but rather a hope that his or her silence will yield a benefit at some future date.

Even though circumstantial and situational political corruption are not generally covered in news stories nor prosecuted by law enforcement authorities, they have a significant corrosive effect on both society and the political processes and are no less corrupt in their nature than the traditional form or political corruption. Unfortunately there is no way to measure situational or circumstantial corruption since they may not constitute unlawful acts but rather immoral or unethical acts that do not rise to the level of a prosecutable offense. Because of the inability to measure all corrupt acts of a political nature, corruption ratings seldom, if ever, reflect the true nature of a government's state of integrity. The "science" of corruption measurement may in fact be more of an art form than an empirical process. Even when users of corruption measurement tools employ the use of multiple sources of case studies, data and analysis, a true measurement cannot be attained simply because most politically corrupt acts, those of a passive, circumstantial or situational nature, are seldom brought to light and therefore cannot be counted by those performing the measurement studies.

Traditional measurement tools compare population of a political or governmental entity against the number of indictments or convictions set down within that jurisdiction. This precise standard, however, ignores much of the corruption activity because the very nature of the activity renders it unprosecutable. In 2008, The United Nations Development Programme's (UNDP's) Oslo Governance Centre to Global Integrity published A User's Guide to

Measuring Corruption. It notes that "Virtually every generator of governance or corruption indicators says it is measuring 'governance' or 'corruption,' with little clarity regarding what is actually being assessed." The Guide continues, "The term "corruption" has been applied to such a wide variety of beliefs and practices that pinning down the concept is difficult." Both input and output-based indicators have been deemed equally weak in this regard. Yet, even new approaches that were developed to map "out the power dynamics among actors and institutions" have failed to provide clarity.

For the one type of corruption that can be most adequately measured, active traditional corruption, the best available yardstick is the conviction rate for prosecutable offenses relative to the state's population. Under this measurement, various states were rated and even among the agencies performing the measurements, the results vary widely.

Despite Rhode Island's reputation for being the most corrupt state in the United States, results of many studies show that that may not be the case. Many studies do not even rank Rhode Island in the top ten. Virginia and Florida, the top two most corrupt states in the union, according to one study, run away with that honor. According to research data presented by Thomas Schlesinger and Kenneth J. Meier in a study of political corruption in the United States, each of those states had a rate of federal misconduct convictions per 100 elected officials exceeding ten. In other words, in a 10-year national study done between 1986 and 1995, Virginia and Florida each had more than 10% of their elected officials convicted on federal misconduct charges.[2] Rhode Island, by comparison, ranks number eleven in that study with about three percent of its officials being convicted of federal misconduct. That same study indicates that Vermont and New Hampshire were the least politically corrupt states with about 1/10 of 1 percent of those elected officials being convicted of federal misconduct.

Other national studies, taken at different times or examining different corruption criteria, indicate that Rhode Island fares even better than that. According to a 2002 report of the US Department of Justice, Public Integrity Section, public corruption from the years 1993 to 2002 indicate that Rhode Island ranked 20th with a 3.08 ratio of corruption convictions per 100,000 people. The study reported that Rhode Island had 33 convictions against a population of 1,069,725. The states with the highest corruption rate in that study were Mississippi (7.48), North Dakota (7.09) and Louisiana (7.05). The study concludes that the least corrupt states in the nation were Nebraska (0.52) and Oregon (0.59).

Also "in 2002 in Chicago, the Better Government Association (BGA) released what it called the first independent, comprehensive report on integrity in the 50 states – a ranking of all fifty states based on the relative strength of laws that protect against corruption and promote integrity in the operations of state government. The top five states in the BGA Integrity Index were Wisconsin, Rhode Island, Kentucky, Hawaii and California. The bottom five states listed in the study were Louisiana, Alabama, New Mexico, Vermont and South Dakota."[3]

Finally, the Center of Public Integrity's annual State Integrity Investigation lists Rhode Island as the 9th most corrupt state in the United States with New Jersey being first and Georgia coming in as the least corrupt state.

The evidence presented from these three independent studies, completed over a significant span of time, indicate a substantial dichotomy between the public attitude toward Rhode Island corruption and the facts. These studies tend to clearly indicate that Rhode Island is not the most corrupt, or even close to being the most corrupt, state in America

These disparate results are the best evidence of the impossible nature of the ability to measure political corruption. These statistics do not disprove the belief that Rhode Island is the most corrupt state, they merely demonstrate the difficulty in defining political corruption and measuring it with any type of comprehension and definition.

Rather than attempting to measure political corruption for purposes of establishing a ranking of the most corrupt states in America, a task that has thus far proven to be impossible, this book will retell actual cases of Rhode Island political corruption to demonstrate the types of corruption that exist and the effects of that corruption on the very people that public officials are elected or appointed to serve. Although accurate descriptions of actual events, these stories are by no means a totality of political corruption in Rhode Island, but rather a smattering intended for demonstration purposes.

PART I

TRADITIONAL POLITICAL CORRUPTION

Some forms of political corruption are quite obvious and easily identifiable. A bribe or an act of extortion, do not represent a simple breach of ethics or morality. They are overt violations of the public trust. They are illegal acts punishable by time in federal or state prison and/or by the levy of substantial fines and penalties. They represent the most abhorrent acts of personal greed and the most egregious contempt of the leader's fiduciary compact with the governed. Traditional political corruption is nothing short of reprehensible and deserving of the most severe penalties judicial review can appropriate.

Rhode Island has certainly been no stranger to this form of corruption and over the years its newspapers have been filled with accounts of its existence. While examples of Rhode Island's traditional political corruption are many, the few examples recounted here highlight some of the higher profiled cases the Ocean State has endured. Though unique in many respects, each case is also symbolic of the greed and avarice that characterizes such political chicanery. The most convoluted example of political corruption offered in this book is contained in the strange case of Governor Edward DiPrete retold in chapter 3. The accounts of events of the corrupt activity told in that story span almost a decade and encompass so many corrupt acts that a substantial portion of this book is dedicated to its retelling.

1

BUGS IN CITY HALL

Mayor Brian Sarault

Thirty-year old Robert A. Weygand already owned and operated his own landscape architecture business in East Providence when he decided to turn his attention to politics. In 1978 the founder and President of Weygand, Orchich & Christie, Inc. accepted an appointment to the East Providence Planning Board. He enjoyed the pace and the opportunity to offer his expertise in the future development of his city. So it should have surprised none of his colleagues when in 1985 he decided to seek elected political office and announced a run for a seat in Rhode Island's General Assembly. He was elected to the State House of Representatives and took office in January of 1985. In a very short time he established himself as a leader when he engineered passage of the new state Zoning Enabling Act; a comprehensive piece of legislation that essentially rewrote the state's outdated zoning laws.

Representative Bob Weygand as pictured in
the Congressional Pictorial Directory, 106th Congress.

His youthful energy and Kennedyesq appearance escaped no one's notice as he brought together planners, developers and environmentalists, groups traditionally at odds in such matters, in a working committee designed to enlist their services and solicit their expertise in the development of the new laws. Also obvious were his political savvy and leadership skills as he sought and achieved unanimity from this diverse and potentially divisive committee.

Despite his apparent rising star status in the state's Democrat Party, it would be something beyond his wildest imagination that would thrust Bob Weygand into the Rhode Island limelight and make him front page news.

The Democrats had another rising star in their ranks. Forty-Five year old "Pawtucket Mayor Brian Sarault was considered by many to be quite good looking. The dapper and self-assured mayor had been comfortably reelected to a second two-year term in 1990 and was already being mentioned as a possible gubernatorial candidate."[4] Something of a whiz kid, Sarault graduated high school at the age of 16 and moved on to Providence College. He was a classmate of U.S. Senator and presidential candidate Christopher Dodd and Bristol County District Attorney Ronald A. Pina. Sarault graduated Suffolk Law School in 1969 and began his law practice in Rhode Island. He married at age 27 but that union lasted only 8 years. He entered the political world in 1977 winning his first election earning a seat on the Pawtucket City Council.

Brian Sarault

Many years later on a hot July day in 1991, Sarault walked from his office to Main Street to attend a ceremony marking the renovation of an old fountain. "A passer-by paused when he saw Sarault, walked over to the mayor and asked him about the troublesome newspaper headlines. Sarault smiled. It was the kind of question he had heard often since his arrest a month earlier on the charge of extortion....' This fellow named Weygand came along,' Sarault reassured the stranger in a melodic voice. 'I sold him some fund-raiser tickets and somehow he got confused. Don't believe everything you read in the newspapers. I was a lawyer 20 years, and I know better than to try a case in the paper. Just give me my day in court.' "[5]

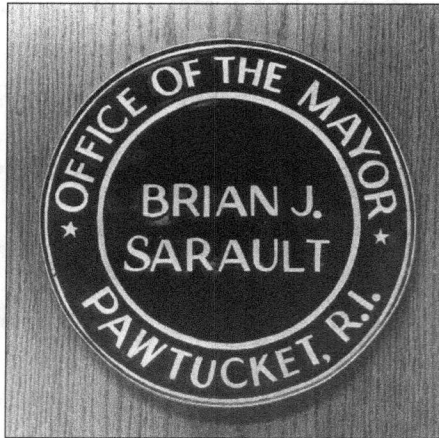

The sign on the door to the mayor's office.

Sarault convinced this man as he had convinced so many others since his arrest that he was innocent. That ability, in part, was why he was such a successful politician. Not only did he have the ability to dismiss his flaws and contradictions, but he was also able to turn them to his political advantage. "Those familiar with Pawtucket politics talk about Sarault's charm, his charisma, and how those traits have given him the ability to negotiate political minefields. 'He's a master at that,' said City Council President Raymond Houle. 'He gives the impression he's being picked on, and he's got this mesmerizing manner. More than anything else, I think that's what propelled him into office.' "6

Sarault's charisma and charm, however, were not enough to hold his marriage together. In 1980, just as he was about to begin his second term on the Council, Sarault's wife Deborah filed for divorce citing "irreconcilable differences" and saying that Brian Sarault "had been 'guilty of extreme cruelty.' "7 As part of the settlement, Sarault had to sell the home he owned with his wife Deborah and purchase a new home for her. He purchased one at 15 Concord St. in Cranston, RI from an elderly woman by name of Irene L. Mulick. Mulick, who was ill and was having trouble paying her bills, agreed to sell the house for $40,000. Sarault was also able to convince Mulick to loan him $15,000 for the down payment and to do so without consulting an attorney or requiring collateral. The terms of the promissory note indicated 12% interest and simply required repayment within 12 months. Mrs. Mulick died in 1985 having never received one penny toward the loan repayment. Not only did he not offer payment, but fourteen months later, just two months after final payment had been due, Sarault visited Mulick, who by now lived with her sister, 84-year old Marion F. Byrnes of Pawtucket, and allegedly asked her to let him borrow more money. Byrnes husband, who overheard the conversation, threw Sarault out. Sarault later denied asking for more money, and said he was visiting Mrs. Mulick to make new payment arrangements.

Mulick filed a civil complaint against Sarault on September 13, 1982. According to court documents, Sarault filed bankruptcy nine days later owing $142,825.32 and claiming assets of $4,073.07. The bankruptcy was resolved in 1985 with Sarault's twelve creditors each taking a share of his assets. "Miss Mulick's estate was repaid just $536.25 of the $15,000 she loaned Sarault. She died seven months before the bankruptcy was settled."[8]

While struggling with his financial issues, Sarault married for the second time. Margaret Mary "Peggy" McNamee, a dental hygienist in Warwick, and Sarault were married on January 22, 1984. Less than one year later, Sarault announced he would run for Mayor. However, as his campaign efforts were unfolding, "his father and younger brother were in federal court in Florida facing fraud charges for allegedly bilking at least $600,000 from borrowers in a loan scheme. Aime Sarault (Brian's father) was eventually acquitted. But Stephen Sarault was found guilty on Feb. 23, 1985. He was sentenced to two years in prison and fined $2,000. He spent most of his time in the Federal Correctional Institution at Loretto in Pennsylvania. Brian Sarault claims to have had a falling out with Stephen and says he never visited his brother in prison."[9] Regardless, the family scandal may have had an adverse affect on the campaign and Sarault lost the election by 352 votes to Henry Kinch.

In 1987, Pawtucket's Mayor Kinch decided not to seek re-election leaving Sarault in a personally bitter battle for the office against Councilwoman Kathleen Magill.

The contest became very personal in nature and was extremely close when Magill made a decision to release records regarding Sarault's bankruptcy and divorce. She argued that a person who couldn't manage his own finances might have trouble managing the finances of a city. But the decision turned out to be a bad one. Sarault portrayed himself as a victim being persecuted by someone with a complete lack of compassion. Sarault won the election capturing 63% of the vote. Along with the good news of his wide margin of victory, Sarault's personal financial fortunes began to turn around. By 1988 Sarault had purchased a $131,000 home in Pawtucket and a condominium in Cape Cod. In addition to his personal good fortunes, Sarault's fundraising reached new heights. Sarault's campaign finance reports disclosed that he raised over $600,000 since deciding to run for Mayor in 1985.

In 1989, Sarault found himself embroiled in another difficult battle for re-election. Sarault spent over $283,000 to win that race and in the process established a new spending record for a city race outside of Providence. He captured 55% of the vote in defeating former Councilman and State Representative Thomas E. Hodge.

A short time later, in August of 1990, the landscape architecture firm of Weygand, Orchlich, & Christie, Inc. was awarded a $43,360 contract to provide landscaping upgrades to Pawtucket's Slater Park. "In March 1991, the city planning department asked the firm...to do more work at the park."[10] So in April 1991, when Weygand received a phone call from Pawtucket Mayor Brian Sarault, he naturally assumed that they would discuss the Park's design. Instead of engaging in a lengthy conversation, however, Sarault simply "asked to meet personally with Weygand to discuss the contract change. Weygand first met with Sarault on April 18th. Saying he needed money for a 'tough election coming up,' Sarault allegedly asked Weygand to inflate the cost of the additional work by $5,000. At that meeting, the mayor turned up the radio and laid out a scenario under which he would get $3,000, and Weygand would keep $2,000."[11] Weygand was stunned. After nine years in business, dealing with municipalities on a regular basis, no one had ever tried to extort money from him. "'In those few seconds,' " Weygand would later say, "'you think about the good and the bad and everything else in between. And the thing that just kept popping up in my mind was: The most important thing to me has been my family and my reputation. I just didn't want to be part of any of this that would affect either one.' "[12] Weygand collected his thoughts and told the mayor he would like to participate, but wouldn't be able to come up with the money all at one time. The mayor suggested that instead of a one-time contribution, Weygand could purchase ten $125.00 tickets to his upcoming fundraiser. That would provide the cover for the first payment of $1,250.

Weygand was troubled but knew what needed to be done. He first conferred with his wife and then his lawyer and General Assembly colleague Frank Gaschen, a close personal friend. That next morning, Weygand called US Attorney Lincoln C. Almond. Shortly thereafter, he went to the Federal Bureau of Investigation and agreed to wear a wire and tape record meetings in Pawtucket City Hall and telephone conversations with Sarault and others that might be related to the park improvements.

The opportunity to make the first recording didn't take long to present itself. On May 8, 1991, "Weygand received a telephone message from Pawtucket City Solicitor Frederick Joslyn. The FBI recorded the call when Weygand returned it and Joslyn asked him the status of the tickets. Weygand told Joslyn that he would deal with the mayor on the tickets. The same day, Weygand set up another meeting with Sarault."[13]

In preparation for the meeting, the FBI gave Weygand $1,250 in marked bills and wired him for sound. On May 15, 1991, Weygand and Sarault met in the mayor's office where Weygand presented Sarault with two contracts, each document containing a different option for padding the contract by $5,000. After selecting one of the options, the parties signed two originals. With Weygand still present, and the FBI listening in, Sarault called city planning director Roger Giraud and "asked if it would be a problem to increase the contract by $5,000. Giraud said it would not, Sarault told Weygand. Weygand gave Sarault the 1,250"[14] and left.

Two days later on May 17th Weygand returned a call he had received from Sarault the previous day. The FBI was listening in when "Sarault asked him how many tickets he intended to use. Weygand said he needed two and the mayor said he would put Weygand down for three and 'use the rest for some of my people.' "[15] Shortly after hanging up, Weygand mailed an invoice for the "additional services" part of the transaction. On the day of the fundraiser, May 21, 1991, FBI agent Nicholas J. Murphy listened to another conversation in which Sarault told Weygand that Giraud, who was in the room next to Sarault, said that Weygand's city check for part of the contract work would be available that week. When the check was not ready by Friday, Weygand called again and was told that Sarault would straighten out the payment to Weygand so he (Sarault) could get the "second half." When asked by Weygand if he was referring to the $1,750, Sarault answered "right."

Weygand was again fitted with a wire and a body microphone on Wednesday, June 12th, before walking into Sarault's office to deliver the second payment of $1,750. It was just before 1:30 in the afternoon. Weygand had been nervous and concerned that Sarault might try to run his hand across Weygand's back to feel for a wire. He was also aware enough to position the recording device elsewhere on his body.

Brian Sarault, accompanied by his wife Peggy, leave federal court following his arraignment for extortion and other related charges.

Weygand and the FBI had anticipated correctly, for as Weygand turned to walk out of Sarault's office just a few minutes later, Sarault patted Waygand's shoulder and quickly ran his hand all the way down Weygand's back to the waist. Shortly after Weygand left Sarault's office two men who identified themselves as FBI agents walked in and presented Sarault with arrest warrants for extortion, mail fraud and accepting an illicit payment as an agent of an organization that gets federal funds. The office was searched and Sarault was taken to Federal Court in Providence where he pled not guilty before U.S. Magistrate Judge Jacob Hagopian. Sarault's wife Peggy stood by his side. "The FBI and state police detectives, meanwhile, executed search warrants at Pawtucket City Hall."[16]

Sarault, who on June 3, 1991 had announced that he would run for a third term on a reform platform now found himself looking at up to 35-years in prison and $750,000 in fines. Rather than facing 34-year old City Councilman William Lynch, son of former Pawtucket Mayor Dennis Lynch and Sarault's harshest council critic, he would be facing a judge. Later that night, Sarault's lawyer, Charles J. Rogers, Jr., told reporters that the charges were nothing more than allegations and the mayor had no intention of resigning.

Despite Rogers' pronouncement, and Sarault's claims of innocence, Sarault's problems continued to mount. Allegations surfaced that city money collected from the payment of tickets resulting from "an ingenious – though controversial – way to raise revenues through an aggressive police crackdown on speeders, called the Pawtucket Accident Reduction Enforcement (PARE) program, were being diverted to Sarault's campaign account. The crackdown, which was launched in June 1989, nailed more than 22,000 speeders in the last year (1990) and raked in about $1.4 million. An outside auditing firm hired by the City Council began investigating the program which was believed to involve up to $600,000 of missing funds.

In addition, on August 14, 1991, a federal grand jury handed up a second extortion-related indictment against Sarault for a 1990 attempt to solicit a $5,000 kickback from an engineering firm seeking a contract with the City's Public Buildings Authority. Sarault maintained his innocence and refused to step down, although he did declare that he would no longer seek a third term as Mayor of Pawtucket.

Brian Sarault enters the courthouse to enter a plea following his arrest for extortion, mail fraud, and accepting an illicit payment as an agent of an organization that gets federal funds.

The two cases were merged and were scheduled for trial in the fall of 1991 despite a defense motion plea to keep them separate. Kevin J. O'Dea, arguing for the defense said that the jury might confuse the two cases. "Prosecutor Edwin J. Gale countered that the two alleged criminal acts were 'identical schemes' that occurred less than 10 months apart. Judge Torres agreed with Gale and denied the motion.

On October 4, 1991, a federal grand jury indicted Sarault and 39-year old Louis S. Simon, the city's acting public works director, on charges that they extorted $10,500 in kickbacks from two city contractors hired to make improvements to city playgrounds and parks. "The indictment alleged that Sarault and Simon extorted a $3,500 kickback from Walter R. Lenartowicz and his business, Pawtucket Fence and Iron Works, after the business was awarded a $33,508 contract in August 1989. In a second indictment, Simon was accused of extorting $7,000 from Domenic A. Rucco and Thomas S. Borkowski. Their company, D.A.R.E. Inc., of Rehoboth, MA, was hired as a subcontractor by Seaview Construction Inc. of Providence to perform work worth $229,400 in city parks."[17] The new charges against Sarault included extortion, conspiracy, and the illicit receipt of money by a government official, and the interstate use of a telephone facility to further extortion and mail fraud. These charges were also combined with the previous charges resulting in a total of 18 extortion-related charges. Convictions on all counts could have put Sarault behind bars for 115 years as well as forcing him to pay $2.5 million in fines.

Sarault, who still refused to leave office, did start to lose the support of his peers. Council President Raymond

W. Houle, once a close ally of Saraults, called him a "total disgrace." Perhaps more disgraceful was the fact that Simon was suspended while Sarault still held office.

In early November 1991, Robert E. Metivier was elected to succeed Sarault as Pawtucket's mayor. On November 7, 1991, at about 9:30 A.M., Brian J. Sarault and his wife Peggy gathered about 25 City workers in an old courtroom next to his City Hall office and told them that he would resign his office about two months prior to the expiration of his current term. In a carefully worded one-page statement issued to the press, Sarault said, "I am truly and deeply sorry for what I have caused, and wish only that I had not done so. To those people who gave to me their support, loyalty and trust, I say I am deeply sorry and hope that I can someday earn your forgiveness."[18] While Sarault stopped short of admitting guilt, his resignation fueled speculation that he had worked out a plea bargain with prosecutors. Council President Houle, who had taken over the day-to-day city operations since June, prepared to take the oath of office as interim-mayor until Metivier's term would begin. ' "It took him this long to do the honorable thing, but at least he finally did it,' Houle said. 'This gives us the opportunity to put the house in order before Bob Metivier comes in.' "[19]

The next day, Sarault pleaded guilty in U.S. District Court, to accepting or soliciting more than $300,000 in bribes and kickbacks while he was mayor. Simon pleaded guilty to one count of extortion. Both men agreed to cooperate with federal investigators. A sentencing date was set for January 24, 1992. US Attorney Lincoln C. Almond, who up to this point refused public comment on the Sarault investigation, finally broke his silence saying that just about anyone who held a high level position within Sarault's administration is a likely target of the on-going investigation.

Brian Sarault and his wife Peggy hurry into a waiting car after Brian's sentencing for extortion, and accepting or soliciting bribes and kickbacks, totaling more than $300,000 while serving as mayor of Pawtucket.

Despite the admission, the City Council wasn't satisfied. They hired a Boston lawyer, R. Robert Popeo, a fraud investigation specialist who, a few years later, would defend Governor Edward DiPrete's son Dennis in his public corruption case, to investigate Sarault's dealings and issue a report to the City. On November 19, 1991, the Council received the 40-page report that said in part, "Brian J. Sarault's administration regularly circumvented bidding procedures to steer city contracts to campaign contributors and companies paying kickbacks." Even companies submitting the lowest bids were often paid, at Sarault's direction, thousands of dollars above their original estimates. The report urged the investigation of former City Solicitor Fred E. Joslyn for possible theft of city services and breach of duties. The report also said that city employees regularly violated the City Charter by soliciting campaign contributions for Sarault on city time. The report urged that the city sue vendors and city officials, including Sarault, under the federal Racketeering Influenced and Corrupt Organizations (RICO) Act. Houle and Metivier said that the city would more than likely follow that recommendation.

A shackled Sarault entering court to testify
on money missing from the city of Pawtucket.

On Friday, January 31, 1992, Judge Ernest Torres sentenced Sarault to five-and-a-half-years in prison for his role in the extortion ring. Although the sentence could have been as much as twenty years in prison, prosecutors argued for a sentence of only 4 years, 9 months citing the fact that Sarault was cooperating with the investigation. "In imposing the longer term, Judge Ernest C. Torres, said there were many victims of the scheme: 'taxpayers, the legitimate vendors who couldn't get work because they wouldn't play ball, the citizens of Pawtucket who found their trust in government eroded' and 'honest public officials who served the public interest but are now under the cloud of suspicion."[20]

Louis Simon was sentenced to 46 months in federal prison for his part in the scheme.

How could a charismatic elected official with a promising future in politics go from being a hardworking lawyer with an unblemished record to a power-hungry Pawtucket Mayor demanding bribes and kickbacks? No one that knew him well would have predicted he was capable of such behavior. A reporter said Sarault offered this explanation. "Once he took office as mayor it was a different story: People who wanted to do business with the city promised to make it worthwhile for him, and he succumbed to the temptation, soliciting contributions and bribes. 'In the Mayor's job, you just get caught up in this fundraising activity. I got caught up like I never should have got caught up.' He said."[21]

Sarault offered a similar explanation in an attempt to regain the law license he had lost when he was disbarred on December 12, 1991 after pleading guilty to one count of racketeering. Pleading his case to a "three-member panel of Massachusetts Board of Bar Overseers, which has the power to reinstate him as a lawyer despite the racketeering conviction and the five-and-a-half years he spent behind bars. In a letter to the Board, Governor Almond, who prosecuted Sarault when he served as US Attorney, wrote, 'In light of his conduct as a public official and his subsequent incarceration for racketeering, Mr. Sarault has established that he does not have the moral or ethical strength to represent members of the public in any capacity.' "[22]

On July 29, 2002, Justice Sosman of the Supreme Judicial Court of Suffolk County, MA., denied the reinstatement noting that the "petitioner failed to prove that he has the moral qualifications required for admission to practice law and that his resumption of practice will not be detrimental to the integrity or standing of the bar, the administration of justice or the public interest."[23]

Lt. Governor Bob Weygand in 1993.

In 1992 Bob Weygand successfully sought to become Rhode Island's 65th Lt. Governor and served in that position until 1997 when he ran for an open seat in the United States House of Representatives. He served in the US House for four years before challenging Lincoln Chafee for a seat in the United States Senate, the one election Weygand did not win.

2

REAL ESTATE IS NOT
THE ONLY THING FOR SALE

Lincoln Town Administrator Jonathon F. Oster

The Saturday morning of February 16, 2002 was fairly cold. For Rhode Island, it was a typical winter day. For Lincoln Administrator, Jonathan F. Oster, it was not that much different than most Saturdays. As he so often did, Oster was heading to his private law office at 1525 Louisquisset Pike. Prior to his election as Town Administrator, Oster spent countless hours at his office meeting with clients and shuffling through papers. By most accounts, he had built a fairly successful law practice. On this particular Saturday he was planning to meet with his old friend and fundraiser, Robert Picerno. But as Oster would soon learn, nothing on this day would be like any other day in his life. Before nightfall, Oster would begin a six-year battle to protect his reputation and preserve his freedom.

Jonathan Oster in happier times.

Though Oster had been involved in politics for only a few years, he was no stranger to the game. He grew up in a political environment as his father had served as the town's very first town administrator. The younger Oster earned his bachelors' degree at the University of Rhode Island in 1973, his masters from the same school in 1976, and his law degree from Suffolk University in 1981. By 1996 he was a partner in the firm of Oster & Sawyer and was already actively involved in the community having previously served as president of the Cumberland/Lincoln Rotary. He was also a Trustee of the Town's Land Trust and co-coordinator of the Lincoln Watershed Watch Program. In that year he made his entry into elected politics with a successful run for the Rhode Island State Senate. Already a successful lawyer, Senator-elect Oster, who was married and had two children, was sworn into his first political office in January 1997.

*The Limerock Center - Jonathan Oster's law office
at 1525 Louisquisset Pike.*

Following two short, relatively uneventful terms in the State Senate, Democrat Oster decided to challenge Republican Burton Stallwood, Lincoln's Town Administrator since 1972, for the town's highest elected office. Robert R. Picerno played a key fundraising role in this election. According to Michael Hill, a Cumberland accountant and campaign treasurer for all three of Oster's election efforts, Picerno raised $10,655, or more than 25% of the $43,284 total that Oster raised in his 2000 run for town administrator.

Oster was a scrappy fighter, and despite long odds, he managed to edge out Stallwood in a tense and hotly contested political battle. The hard feelings created during the election didn't end on election day, however, and Oster's planned inauguration was delayed one month, to January 2001, after the State's highest court granted an injunction that was filed by Stallwood. The two politicians had a dispute over when Stallwood's term should end and Oster's begin.

The Lincoln Town Hall in Lincoln, RI.

L. Robert Smith, who was recruited by Picerno to do some interim engineering work for the Town's Planning Board, said Picerno served on Oster's transition team and helped Oster put his office together in early 2000.

One of Oster's first acts as town administrator was to pay "almost $1,000 to an electronic surveillance company to scour Town Hall for illegal listening devices. It was a display charged as much with arrogance as paranoia and no bugs were found."[24] Oster justified his actions at the time by saying, "there 'were a number of issues that raised the level of concern. There was some behavior going on in office just prior to the other administrator leaving.' Given that, Oster said, 'we thought it prudent to conduct a search."[25]

Perhaps this initial behavior should have been a premonition of things to come. But other than the most vocal of his political opponents, no one really seemed to pay too much attention to his actions. Many politicians understand that the public is apathetic and inattentive. That apathy, in fact, is one of the reasons that corruption flourishes.

Oster settled right in and began addressing several of the routine issues that confront an administrator on a daily basis - examination of expenditures and tax revenues, the appointment of qualified department heads and an evaluation of existing programs and policies.

He also addressed some matters that were not so routine. On January 11, 2001, just days after taking office, Oster's friend and political confidant, Robert R. Picerno, asked businessman Robert J. Campellone, "if he wanted to buy the H&H Screw Co. property on Route 116"[26] in Lincoln.

The town had taken title to the property in 1991 for taxes owed. No one purchased it at the tax sale because the property was known to have significant environmental problems. The site contained an undetermined amount of

industrial waste that an old report issued by the State's
Department of Environmental Management estimated
would cost between $400,000 and $2 million to clean up.
Although Banneker Industries had occupied the property
for the past seven years, they had never paid a penny to
the town for rent. When Oster inquired about the arrangement, the once cordial relationship between Banneker and
the town soured.

Campellone, an automobile dealer, had known Picerno for at least a year before Oster's election and the two
had developed a close business relationship. In late 1999,
Campellone sold Picerno a car that included a free alarm
system and a free set of tires. He also included the extended
use of his dealer plates. Although only dealership owners,
corporate officers or their salespeople normally use dealer
plates, state law allows the purchaser of a new vehicle to
use them for up to 20 days. This allows a buyer some time
to register the car and pay Rhode Island's 7% sales tax. Allowing Picerno to use the plates for more than a year ena-
bled him to postpone payment of the sales tax on the
$22,000 vehicle as well as to avoid payment of the town
taxes that would normally have been assessed.

Now Picerno was offering Campellone the H&H
property on behalf of the town, a good place Picerno
thought, for Campellone to locate his car dealership. However, Campellone was offering only $50,000 for the site, a
price that most agreed was too low. Eventually, "Campellone agreed he would pay the town $105,000 for tax title
to the six-acre property and pay Picerno $25,000 in cash.
Campellone seemed a bit anxious to close the property and
take title and was dismayed when he learned that there
would be a delay. Responding to Campellone's question

about the timing, Picerno said at one point 'we can't move too quickly; my guy's only been in ten days,' a reference, Campellone said he assumed, to the recently inaugurated Oster."[27] Campellone, however, expected that the closing would take place by January's end.

For Picerno, this might have been the easiest money he ever made. He would soon learn, however, that even easy money takes some work. The deal dragged. Winter turned to spring and still no closing. In June 2001, an impatient Campellone called Oster directly to determine the status of his "bid." Oster "told him it had to be approved by the Town Council and that Picerno 'is not lying to you.' "[28] During this conversation, Campellone never told Oster that he paid Picerno $25,000 although it is certainly clear that Oster knew of Picerno's involvement in the transaction. But interestingly enough, after the phone call, the deal started to move along quickly. Picerno brought a letter to Campellone to sign regarding his interest in the property, and Oster prepared tax documents and argued to the Town Council that the deal should be accepted.

But the letter that Picerno and his lawyer, Donald Lembo, presented Campellone with "would create a partnership of him (Campellone), Lembo and Picerno to own the property."[29] This took Campellone by surprise because he wasn't looking for partners, especially partners who would not be participating in the financing of the property. Feeling less enthusiastic, but still interested in the deal, Campellone asked his attorney, Joseph DeAngelis, to review the documents. DeAngelis advised Campellone not to proceed, saying of the deal, "it stinks."[30]

Following his attorney's advice, Campellone "told Picerno he was out and wanted his bribe back. To convince

Picerno to refund it, he told him he had tape-recorded one of their conversations about the payoff."[31] Not sure that he was telling the truth, but not wanting to chance finding out, Picerno eventually made a partial repayment "with a $15,000 check made out to Campellone from Major Construction Associates, a company doing business with the town. Major Construction is owned by Robert Gelfuso,"[32] someone who would eventually play a prominent role in the transaction.

Around this same time, David Wayne Daniel, a West Warwick contractor, was working to complete his contractual obligations to build a new concession stand and bathhouse, and to make other improvements to the Fairlawn playground in Lincoln. The relatively small job was being paid with a $150,000 federal grant. According to Daniel, "he and his crews were regularly pestered by town officials who complained about the quality and pace of the work. Daniel was also called to three Friday morning meetings in a row in Oster's office, where the main business, according to Daniel, was 'jumping on my back.' "[33]

While he was berated for the delays, many were not his fault and were certainly not of his doing. One of the problems Daniel encountered was that the playground was located near a wetland requiring a special permit that the town was expected to obtain, but didn't. At one point, Daniel was told to relocate the bathrooms they were set to build, but the town changed its mind after the hole was dug. Daniel had to bury the hole.

Federal Funds Coordinator, Stephen Balestra, was the most frequent visitor to the construction site. Gelfuso complained that Balestra, along with Picerno, pressured him to inflate his billing statements and kick back the over-charges to them. Parks and Recreation Director Paul Prachniak and Public Works Director David T. Harrison also regularly visited the site. These visits made Daniel nervous but he dealt with it. Then, on the Monday follow-ing "the third Friday meeting in Oster's office, one in which Daniel told Oster that he wanted to be on his team, Plan-ning Board member Picerno showed up at the site. "'He asked me how things were going and I told him they're busting my...and he started to laugh a little slyly' Daniel said. 'Picerno then took out a pack of 100 Oster fundraiser tickets worth $50 a piece - $5,000 total – and asked if he, Daniel, could take care of them. I said, 'If you can get those...guys off my back,' Daniel said he told Picerno. 'He said, No problem.' "[34] Picerno then described the H&H Screw deal in an obvious effort to spark Daniel's interest.

Rather than paying the full $5,000 requested, Dan-iel presented Picerno a check for $4,750 "because he had already donated $250 to the Oster campaign, and he didn't want to double pay."[35] Picerno wouldn't accept the check and told Daniel, "I'm going to need it in a nicer way."[36] Dan-iel knew that meant he wanted cash, which he later pre-sented to a grateful Picerno.

The name of Daniel's company was Major Construc-tion Associates and his partner was none other than Robert Gelfuso, the same man that had provided the $15,000 check used by Picerno to partially return the bribe he re-ceived from Campellone. Shortly after the playground ex-change, the pressure ceased and Oster commended Daniel on a job well done with the site.

Picerno used the Administrator's office to enhance his own economic status. Many of his actions were self-serving and the more that people visiting Town Hall saw the ease with which he could gain access to the Administrator, the more the perception of his power was exaggerated. He was frequently seen on the rear deck of Town Hall, the deck that "had access to the rest of Town Hall through a sliding door into a conference room that was next to Oster's private office. It was rarely, if ever, used by the public."[37]

In 2001, Picerno's wife Joyce filed suit against the Town of Lincoln "contesting the way the town assessed taxes on the family's Preakness Drive home. She challenged the method the town used to assess taxes from 1998-2000, refusing to pay about $22,000 in property taxes over those three years, some before Oster took office."[38] Emerson Johnson, the Tax Assessor at the time, wanted to settle the suit for $11,000, but Oster said he felt comfortable enough in the friendship to convince Picerno to agree to $15,000. According to a secret tape recording of the November 20, 2001 Town Council executive session, Former Assistant Town Solicitor William Dickie suggested that the Council allow Picerno to pay $15,000 of the $22,000 tax bill owed because the $7,000 loss would be less expensive than litigation. The Council voted to support Dickie's recommendation, but after only a few days, Councilman Dean Lees, Jr., who abstained in the executive session vote, questioned the manner in which the suit was being settled and threatened to contact the state police. It was only after Lees' threat that Dickie said he conducted additional research and found that the Picernos "hadn't filed a timely appeal with the assessor, or paid the taxes, both requirements that must be met before a suit can be filed. He said he then recommended that the Council fight the suit."[39] Regarding the filing of the appeals, Dickie said he relied on the word of the tax assessor. He also said he had assumed that if the taxes had not been paid, the assessor would have informed him of that. However, the law regarding the filing of timely appeals and payment of taxes was contained in the document that Dickie filed before the executive session. Dickie said that the document was boilerplate and that he "hadn't specifically read the statute the document he filed cited."[40]

Leon A. "Lee" Blais served Oster from January to June 2001, first as a consultant, then as the Director of Public Works, and eventually as the Assistant Town Administrator. Blais was concerned about more than the perception of power that easy access afforded Picerno. He was uncomfortable from the start that Picerno "seemed to have the run of Town Hall."[41]

Picerno had served on Oster's transition team – a position that extended for several months. It is fair to say that the two were very close. Upon taking office, Oster assigned Picerno an office next to his and provided access to what may have been a private entrance in Oster's personal office. From this vantage point, Picerno interviewed staff personnel and did other work for Oster.

Blais continued to warn Oster about letting Picerno enter into areas of Town Hall that were not accessible to the public. He explained that he was troubled by Picerno's behavior and recommended that Oster stop associating with him. Despite his warnings, Blais would frequently see Oster and Picerno together at the Lodge, a local tavern frequented by town politicians. One day, while Oster was sitting at the Lodge's bar Blais approached him. "I basically used a raspy voice and characterized Mr. Picerno as Darth Vader" Blais said. "Oster said he would 'take steps' to rein in Picerno, but invariably, Picerno would return."[42] Oster justified the relationship by telling Blais that Picerno was an integral part of his campaign organization, capable of raising large sums of money and rallying the town's Italo-American population on his behalf.

But Blais's fears seemed to be founded in fact. In the fall of 2001, two private citizens, filed two separate state police complaints involving Picerno, alleging "that they had been approached about paying a bribe to a town official."[43] The subsequent investigation would involve "the first-ever state court authorized wiretap into public corruption."[44]

At a meeting held on Thursday, February 14, 2002, the state police had the video and audiotape running when David Wayne Daniel and Picerno discussed the details of the bribe payments. Gelfuso was to pay Picerno $25,000 for the tax title document that would allow Daniel and his partner to take over the land.

Wired for sound by the state police, Gelfuso did meet with Picerno at Stuffie's Restaurant in North Providence. Police took photographs as Gelfuso handed over a bulging envelope containing a $5,000 partial payment to Picerno when the two were in the parking lot.

But the payment plan morphed several times. During a taped conversation that took place on December 4, 2001, Picerno suggested that instead of cash, Picerno could pay Gelfuso $75,000 for a piece of property worth $100,000. Daniel would make a payment of $15,000 to cover legal fees. He would also pay the town $105,000 as a purchase price for the property. "There were no formal names in Picerno's patter; it was 'Frankie' and 'Bobby.' 'Fifty green' was $50,000. He would hint and imply, using phrases like – 'you know what I'm saying?' – rather than say things directly. And there were repeated hints at nebulous future deals."[45]

At the time of this meeting, Picerno was serving on the Lincoln Planning Board, a body that was able to determine the fortunes of a developer with a "yes" or "no" vote. During the session, Picerno alluded to future deals, spoke of lessons from prior dealings and boasted of his clout while talking about failed deals that he could have saved. They also spoke of potential tenants for the property. They included Campellone's car dealership and a 7-Eleven store that Campellone had talked about building. Picerno told Daniel he could match or pay 10% more than what another contractor could do.

On Friday, February 15, 2002, Gelfuso met with Picerno and delivered the $20,000 bribe balance for the purchase of the H&H property. The payment was made with money that the state police had convinced Citizen's Bank to provide through a cooperative agreement with the bank. Citizen's also provided a phony bank check made out to the Town of Lincoln for $105,000 as the agreed upon payment for the land.

Following that meeting, Campellone was arrested and charged with bribery. He entered a guilty plea and was offered a five-year deferred sentence in exchange for his cooperation against Oster and Picerno.

So, on that cold, winter, Saturday morning of February 16, 2002, Oster and Picerno met for almost an hour. Oster had no way of knowing that Picerno, who had already been arrested on February 14th, was also wearing a police wire. "The meeting started in Oster's office, but moved outside after he told Picerno about how lawyers' offices can be bugged by law enforcement. While they are outside, Oster told Picerno that Gelfuso had been talking to state police, accusing Picerno of extorting money from Gelfuso's partner Daniel in exchange for getting town inspectors to ease up on their inspections of a job site the contractors had in town."[46] The police also videotaped a portion of the meeting that took place outside the law office. During the meeting, Picerno put an envelope with $10,000 in $100 bills "in a metal mailbox, saying "'All right, that's from Wayne, for that H&H [expletive].' The envelope with the cash was found in Oster's office later in the day when police searched it."[47]

A few hours after their meeting ended, Oster was arrested and charged with two counts of bribery and two counts of conspiracy. His six-year legal odyssey was just beginning. The bribery charges alone could bring a jail term of up to 40 years and fines of up to $100,000.

Oster was quick to proclaim his innocence saying that he would stay in office and fight the bribery charges. His critics were just as quick to call for his resignation. On February 17th, just one day after his arrest, several town officials said that Oster should resign his elected position immediately. "Several questioned whether he could effectively govern the town and whether his continued presence would tarnish Lincoln's generally positive image. 'Should he continue? Given these charges, I say no,' said Town Council President Raymond Dapault,' "[48] Just a week earlier, Depault had announced his intention to oppose Oster in the 2002 Democrat primary.

Even Oster's strong supporters, such as Democrat Councilman Dennis Auclair, agreed that Oster would probably have to resign. Republican Burt Stallwood, whom Oster had taken down in the election of 2000, said, "'it's a big disappointment. The town was always considered one of the best-run in the state.' Noting that his predecessor, Barry J. Farrands, was convicted soon after leaving office, Stallwood said, 'This turns the clock back 30 years.' "[49] Ironically, Stallwood had just been appointed U.S. Marshal.

Jonathan Oster was arrested by state police on February 16, 2002 and charged with two counts of bribery and two counts of conspiracy.

Councilman Dean Lees, Jr., a long-time Oster critic promised court action to prevent Oster from entering Town Hall if he did not resign. He added that the news didn't surprise him because of "what he perceives to be the administration's 'numerous charter and ordinance violations since coming to office.' "[50]

Attorney General Sheldon Whitehouse, who at the time was a candidate for Governor and has since gone on to the United States Senate, said of the case, "Rhode Island residents, who pay some of the highest local taxes in the nation, deserve to be protected by aggressive efforts to root out corruption. Such corruption drives up the cost of services, scares off business and fuels apathy and cynicism, poisoning a system of local government that thrives on citizen involvement. Municipal officials must get the message that the law is watching, and that they face serious trouble if they condone corruption or accept bribes in the course of their official business."[51]

On February 19, 2002, Oster told reporters that he was innocent of the charges against him. Speaking outside Town Hall Oster said, "I am going to have an opportunity to prove that in court. I have no further comment until then. As any other innocent individual, I'm coming to work to do my job as I was elected to do by the people of the town of Lincoln. I fully intend to fulfill my functions at my job. Thank you very much."[52]

The Town Council was unmoved. That same night they voted unanimously to ask Jon Oster to resign his office. Oster, who is required under the Town Charter to attend all council meetings, did not show up despite having reported to work that day. The Council passed a second resolution asking lawyers to draft a complaint to the State Ethics Commission, a body that has the legal authority to remove Oster from office, a power that the council did not have. Finally, the council voted to hire an independent counsel to review every transaction the town undertook during Oster's term of office.

Over the course of the next month, several town officials were subpoenaed to appear before a statewide grand jury called to investigate government corruption in Lincoln. Investigators also subpoenaed municipal records from several different departments of town government and state police questioned several key town officials.

In 2004, the Picerno and Oster cases were separated. Picerno pleaded no contest to four counts of soliciting bribes and three counts of conspiracy to solicit bribes. He was sentenced to eight years, three to serve, at the Adult Correctional Institution (ACI) in Cranston, Rhode Island.

Over the next several years, lawyers wrangled over legal motions. Motions to exclude certain evidence from trial and motions to prohibit certain witnesses from testifying. One motion was to suppress evidence obtained through what was alleged to be an unlawful search and seizure that turned up four guns, a .380-caliber handgun, an Ingram 9mm\.45-caliber Mac 10 automatic machine gun, a 12-gauge shotgun and a .22 caliber rifle that were found in Oster's office. Finally, "after several years of pretrial appeals over admissibility of evidence and trial procedure that included an appeal to the state Supreme Court, Oster's trial was scheduled to begin in early January 2008."[53]

Part of the defense strategy became apparent even in pretrial hearings. Clearly, the strategy would be to "attack the credibility of Picerno. Oster's lawyer, C. Leonard O'Brien, called Picerno a liar at more than one pre-trial hearing and in late November 2007 used a disclosure request to try to further tarnish the reputation of what he called the state's core witness. He asked the judge to order the state to specify what Picerno would be testifying to during the trial, saying Picerno had given differing accounts of some events in police interviews and during other hearings."[54]

In January 2008 Superior Court Associate Justice Gilbert V. Indeglia issued his final pre-trial motion ruling paving the way for the long awaited trial to begin. But on February 5, 2008, just 3 days after it began, the trial came to a halt again as two jurors came down with the stomach flu. The one-day delay didn't seem to disrupt the state's momentum, however, as the jury heard damaging testimony against Oster for several consecutive days.

Finally, on February 19, 2008, the 12-member jury was ready to begin deliberating "on whether ex-Lincoln Town Administrator Jonathon F. Oster is guilty of bribery and conspiracy or just bad judgment in his choice of friends."[55] But first, Judge Indeglia explained to the jurors "that if a criminal conspiracy existed, that in itself is a crime. The state wouldn't have to prove a bribe was ever paid, only that Picerno and Oster schemed to get it. All members of a conspiracy are culpable for the acts of other conspirators whether they knew what they were doing or not. One conspirator could even order another not to commit a specific crime, but if the other did it anyway, both are equally liable."[56]

On Thursday, February 21, 2008, little more than two days into their deliberations, the jury returned, and, "After listening to a case that relied heavily on tapes of Picerno's conversations with bribery targets and with Oster, found the former state senator guilty of two counts of bribery and two counts of extortion for actions he took while town administrator from 2000 – 2002."[57]

Judge Indeglia set Oster's sentencing for May 8, 2008. At that time, he would be allowed to sentence Oster to a maximum of 20 years in prison on each bribery charge, and 10 years on each conspiracy count; a total of 60 years. Oster's attorney, C. Leonard O'Brien immediately promised an appeal and Oster was released pending sentencing.

Friday morning, less than a day after his guilty verdict, 56-year old Oster drove to his Louisquisset Pike law office just as he did on most other days. He entered his second floor office at about 7:00 A.M., the same office where his friend, Robert Picerno, had betrayed him 6 years earlier. He walked into the conference room, held a gun to his head and pulled the trigger.

Oster's suicide stunned the community – maybe as much as the charges against him and the guilty verdict did. "Attorney General Patrick C. Lynch, whose office had won the conviction, said, 'this is a tragedy upon a tragedy and, obviously, a heartbreaking loss for Mr. Oster's family and loved ones. I offer them our sincerest sympathies."[58] Many other elected officials expressed shock and spoke of better days with their friend Jonathon Oster.

The suicide had a devastating impact on the jurors as well. Noting that, "he could not recall a case where a defendant killed himself so soon after a verdict,"[59] Superior Court Presiding Justice Joseph F. Rodgers, Jr. offered all 12 jurors and 4 alternates counseling with a specialist with the RI Critical Incident Stress Management Team. At least 14 of the 16 jurors took advantage of the offer as did Judge Indeglia, defense attorney Bethany Macktaz, prosecuting attorney William Ferland and Attorney General Patrick Lynch.

The entire tragedy that is the story of Jonathan Oster was to have one more ironic twist of legal fate. As a result of a unique Rhode Island statute, a convicted person who dies prior to sentencing is considered to have died without guilt. Guilt, in other words, is conferred only upon completion of sentence imposition by a judge. In that sense, Jonathan Oster, having been lawfully convicted by a jury of his peers on all four felony counts charged against him, left this world one day after his conviction, an innocent man.

3

CASH IN THE DUMPSTER

Governor Edward DiPrete

Providence Journal investigative reporters and staff writers Tracy Breton, Mike Stanton, David Herzog, and W. Zachary Malinowski spent hundreds of hours scouring through tens of thousands of pages based heavily upon court documents and records related to the DiPrete case. Collectively, they provided in-depth coverage of the case in real time. This chapter is based heavily upon their research and the work they produced and published in a series written for The Providence Journal *by them.*

There are occasions when an unscrupulous activity in the private sector can spill over into the public sector creating an environment rife for political scandal, a sort of "perfect storm" for corruption. Perhaps this is one way to recount the saga of Governor Edward DiPrete.

Edward DiPrete, just three years after leaving office, became the first Governor of Rhode Island to be charged with corruption. The investigation started four years before that, in 1990, and resulted from the discovery of a $13 million bank embezzlement scheme orchestrated by Joseph Mollicone, the bank's President. The crime would later be described as the event responsible for setting off "Rhode Island's worst financial crisis since the Great Depression."

The story of this scandal involves many different players and events each intimately intertwined with the DiPrete story. Like pieces of a jigsaw puzzle, each fragment contributes to the ultimate disposition of the scandal. Recounting each element of this tale sequentially will help bring into focus the eventual charges against Governor Edward DiPrete.

◆————————————————◆

Joe Mollicone – Providence Banker and Entrepreneur –And His Partner Rodney Brusini

Thirty-four year old lawyer J. Richard Ratcliffe was one of Attorney General James E. O'Neil's first appointments to the newly created 5-member Special Prosecutions unit of the Attorney General's office. With a focus on white-collar crime, formation of the unit was long overdue and was already overburdened with potential cases when Ratcliffe accepted the appointment. He was investigating a case involving the Pastor of St. Anthony's Church in North Providence who was accused of embezzling some $200,000 from the collection plate and bingo money from the parish family when the call came from O'Neil regarding the alleged embezzlement of $13 million from Heritage Loan & Investment Co. by its President, Joseph Mollicone. Later that day, after confronting Mollicone, O'Neil "ordered a grand jury investigation. A week later, on November 8, 1990, Joseph Mollicone vanished,"[60] just two days after DiPrete lost his bid for a fourth, two-year term as Governor.

Less than two weeks following Mollicone's disappearance, the lame duck Governor closed Heritage Loan & Investment Co., but it was too late. Mollicone's actions and the bank's collapse "drained its insurer, the private Rhode Island Share and Deposit Indemnity Corp. (RISDIC). And, the draining of RISDIC imperiled the savings of several hundred thousand depositors at a total of 45 Rhode Island banks and credit unions."[61] Despite pleas from Attorney General O'Neil that it was a conflict of interest due to the potential involvement of top DiPrete aids, DiPrete ordered an investigation by the state police. In Rhode Island, such an investigation falls under the jurisdiction of the Governor's office.

Just as the RISDIC revelations were uncovering how a corrupt political system and a corrupt banking system can nourish each other, those with insider knowledge quietly began to systematically withdraw their money from the affected institutions. "On December 30, 1990, two days before Governor DiPrete left office, the directors of the now-drained Rhode Island Share and Deposit Indemnity Corp. voted themselves out of business. RISDIC's president ... went straight from the meeting to pull his money out of a RISDIC-insured bank before the vaults slammed shut."[62] This is an opportunity that ordinary Rhode Islanders could not take advantage of since the RISDIC proceedings were kept quiet. As a result, many bank board members, some of whom were politically connected as well, were charged with crimes in separate investigations of the RISDIC scandal. Two days later, on the day of Governor Bruce Sundlun's inauguration, the RISDIC banks were closed per order of the new Governor, separating "hundreds of thousands of people from their savings."[63]

Prospect Heights view of the State House where the newly elected governor closed many of the banks and credit unions insured by the Rhode Island Share and Deposit Indemnity Corporation (RISDIC) sparking the biggest banking crisis in RI's recent history.

At just about the same time, an employee of the state Department of Employment Security phoned the

Attorney General's office complaining that some of the Governor's "people" were pressuring him to enter into a lease for the Jesse Metcalf Building in downtown Providence, a building that had been purchased and rehabilitated in 1988 by Joseph Mollicone and his partner Rodney M. Brusini. Brusini was a long-time friend of DiPrete and once acted as his chief fundraiser. Mollicone owned several buildings, many of which were leased by departments of state government. However, for greedy insiders, it apparently wasn't enough that Employment Security had already moved into the Metcalf Building in 1990, Mollicone now wanted the state to rent the 5th floor as well, space, according to *Providence Journal* investigative reporters, the state didn't even need.

Paul Valliere, the Director of Finance for the Department of Employment Security, told the Attorney General that it was his boss, John S. Renza, an associate from the days when DiPrete served as Mayor of Cranston, that introduced him to Mollicone and Brusini at a meeting intended to provide inside information regarding the Department's rental needs to the Metcalf Building owners.

Not only did the state wind up renting the 5th floor space for more money than the landlords were originally asking for, but the owners then presented a $350,000 bill for renovations to the space that the state never authorized. The state paid the bill anyway over the objections of Valliere who was told that he was not a "team player."

"Despite resistance from Valliere and others, the state's rental of the top floor moved forward but eventually fell through when Paul Valliere went to the Attorney General after Mollicone's disappearance."[64] Although citizens protested the bank closings and besieged the Attorney General's office with hundreds of tips on suspicious loans and unscrupulous politicians, the Mollicone lease arrangements remained the prime focus of investigators.

Ratcliffe assembled a team of investigators that included paralegal Peter Blessing who had real estate expertise and Lt. Robert P. Mattos, a State Police Detective with a reputation for latching onto the jugular of those he suspected of wrong doing. Sometime in January of 1991, Blessing came across a check in Mollicone's bank records made out to Anjoorian Carpets in the amount of $875.00. In the memo box were the words "Renza's rug." This was of particular interest because a few days earlier, under Grand Jury questioning by Ratcliffe, Renza couldn't recall the details of the lease, "and denied having spoken to Mollicone or Rodney Brusini before the agency put its rental requirements out to bid."[65]

The new information prompted a second trip by Renza before the Grand Jury. This time, under intense questioning about the rug, Renza collapsed and was taken to Kent County Memorial Hospital where, despite his condition, Lt. Mattos was able to obtain Renza's permission to search his home. Once recovered, Renza was arrested and charged with perjury, bid rigging and obtaining money under false pretenses. Facing an onslaught of legal problems, Renza suddenly remembered everything. "Renza admitted that he had discussed the Metcalf Building lease with co-owners Joseph Mollicone and Rodney Brusini before the state advertised its need for office space. Brusini was pushy, Renza recalled; both he and Mollicone had smugly predicted that their bid would be the lowest.

◆————————————◆

Mathias J. Santos – Top Aide In DiPrete's Department Of Administration, Does DiPrete's Bidding In The Assignment Of A & E Contracts

Renza also told investigators that after his state agency had moved into the Metcalf Building, he was pressured to rent more space, on the top floor. When he protested that the space was unnecessary, Renza said he received a phone call from an angry DiPrete aide. "'God Damn it,' Renza recalled the man's shouting, 'I'm telling you to sign it!'"[66] Renza identified the caller as Mathies Santos, a loyal member of the DiPrete Administration and friend of Brusini and Dennis L. DiPrete, the Governor's son. And this wasn't the only time that Santos, who served on the State Properties Committee, a powerful committee that approved state leases and purchases, pressured someone to sign state leases. "Henry S. Woodbridge, Jr., the director of another job-training agency, told investigators that Santos had screamed at him to move his agency into the building. When Woodridge refused, he told investigators, he received a phone call from Henry Fazzano, DiPrete's chief of staff and another Metcalf Building co-owner. Fazzano ordered Woodbridge to move into the building, but Woodbridge still refused. Fazzano later denied doing anything improper."[67]

Renza wasn't alone with his allegations of political interference. The State Fire Marshall, Everett Ignagni, also revealed details of a phone call he got from a union official telling him how irate Jake Kaplan, a DiPrete contributor, and Dennis DiPrete were that he was resisting attempts to have him rent space in Jake Kaplan's South Providence building. It was also discovered that Santos helped arrange the state's leasing of office space that was paid for even though the state didn't use it. Additionally, Santos was instrumental in obtaining for the owners thousands of dollars in renovations not previously approved by the state. All this after Santos received a $142,500 loan from Heritage Investment & Loan Co. after a bad credit history resulted in a loan rejection by Fleet Bank. Despite these findings, and contrary to the judge's assertions, "the DiPrete-case investigators believed that Santos had been involved in "this overall scheme," as a prosecutor would later refer to the state's rental of Joseph Mollicone's building. But they regarded Santos as merely a messenger – someone who did the DiPrete's' bidding."[68] Even though a judge would later "rule that the state had knowledge of possible criminal activity involving Santos, ranging from conflict-of-interest violations to possible bribery and/or extortion,"[69] prosecutors argued that the behavior was "certainly bad, but not criminal." It appeared that prosecutors were more interested in having Santos as a witness than a suspect. Under an immunity agreement, Santos told investigators that he took his direction regarding leases from Brusini. He also said that both Brusini and Fazzano told him they wanted out of their partnership on the Metcalf Building but could only do so if the building were fully occupied. Santos, in defending his actions also said that the construction bills for which the building partners were reimbursed by the state were legitimate.

The big news, however, came in March of 1991. That's when Santos revealed to investigators that he had also been involved in choosing architects and engineers for state construction projects as well. "Santos said that Dennis DiPrete, the governor's engineer son, would tell Santos whom to hire for projects. Although Dennis DiPrete held no government position, said Santos, Santos followed his instructions because he assumed that the son was communicating his father's wishes."[70]

Apparently, the executive order Governor DiPrete signed during his first year of office creating the selection committee for architects and engineers, on which Santos had served, was a fraud. Santos and others made it clear to the grand jury that it was Edward DiPrete himself who choose the architects and engineers. "It was perfectly clear that it came from him and that he had picked the person," testified Frederick Lippitt, DiPrete's former Director of Administration. "I mean," said Lippitt, "obviously the... system was designed for political patronage, which isn't necessarily... immoral.... You give contracts to those who supported you."[71]

◆────────────────────◆

Frank N. Zaino, Engineer and Political Supporter of Governor DiPrete, Provides Structure to the 'Contracts For Sale' Scheme

With these revelations, and after hearing rumors of state contracts for sale, the investigation turned in a new direction. Investigators found a letter written in 1988 by architect Walter Powers to Dennis DiPrete in which Powers asks Dennis if he could "possibly motivate some positive activity by the state."[72] For the first time, investigators had proof of the Governor's son's involvement. Meanwhile, Lt. Mattos was receiving word from other architects that several other engineers and architects had paid Dennis DiPrete for state contracts. "The tipsters identified Frank Zaino as a key player."[73] Other architects he worked with included David Presbrey, Donald R. Conlon, and Norton Salk. Although Conlon and Salk testified before the Grand Jury that they had done nothing wrong, Mattos believed he had evidence that Salk was a straw donor to DiPrete as he had his assistant make the donation after Salk had reached his legal contribution limit. *(A straw donor is defined as one who makes a contribution on behalf of another person who has already contributed the maximum amount allowed by law. It is illegal in Rhode Island to make a "straw donation".)* Further, Salk instructed the assistant to lie about where the money came from. Additionally, investigators found two of Salk's checks made out to Zaino.

Salk was offered immunity for his truthful testimony and jumped at the opportunity. "Salk now told the Grand Jury that in 1990 he had asked Frank Zaino – whom he'd known for 30 years – to help him get bigger state jobs. Zaino told Salk to come up with $25,000. So, over a six-week period, Salk wrote three checks totaling the requested amount (Zaino later returned one of the checks telling Salk he had paid too much.) Salk didn't get the jobs he wanted. He told the Grand Jury that Zaino had never explicitly promised him the jobs; he had only said come up with $25,000."[74]

The testimony was enough for the Grand Jury to indict Donald Conlon for perjury. Investigators also discovered that money from Conlon's firm was transferred to Zaino's firm, and that Conlon had also given money to friends to donate to the DiPrete campaign once he had reached the legal contribution limit.

Conlon decided to tell the Grand Jury what he knew. According to his version, it started innocently enough. Conlon simply donated to the campaign of a sitting governor. But once he reached the legal limit, "he followed Zaino's instructions and gave money to friends to contribute to the campaign in their names. He also started giving cash to Zaino (something also prohibited under campaign finance law) – generally $4,000 to $5,000 a year. As the demands for money grew, Conlon told the Grand Jury, he opened a line of credit on his house. In 1988, after winning a $430,000 contract to work on the State Training School, Conlon tried to cash a check for $10,000. The teller told him that federal law required her to report any transactions of $10,000 or more. Rather than face that scrutiny, he settled for

$9,950, which he said he gave to Zaino. Zaino told Conlon that he would deliver the cash to Dennis DiPrete, the governor's son. Zaino spoke often of the younger DiPrete as his contact for state jobs, Conlon testified. After Conlon got the Training School contract, Zaino passed along a request from Dennis DiPrete: Conlon should hire Dennis's college roommate as an engineering subcontractor on the job. Conlon did."[75]

Presbrey was the next to testify before the Grand Jury on March 6, 1992. Under a grant of immunity, "he testified that he believed the contributions had been necessary to get state work. And as he gave more money, the jobs rolled in: the new Washington County Court House, the new Block Island airport terminal, the expansion of the Davies Vocational Technical school...The contributions began with checks for tickets to DiPrete fundraising events, which Presbrey would deliver to Rodney Brusini at the F.A. DiPrete Insurance Agency, in Cranston. Brusini was the Governor's chief fundraiser, although Brusini held no government post, Presbrey testified. Presbrey made sure to tell him which state projects he was interested in. Eventually, Presbrey started dealing instead with Frank Zaino. From their conversations, Presbrey gathered that Zaino was reporting to Dennis DiPrete, the Governor's son. But Presbrey, like Salk and Conlon, testified that he never dealt directly with Dennis DiPrete concerning contributions for state contracts. "My sense," Presbrey told a Grand Jury "was that Dennis DiPrete was making the decisions, or Dennis and the Governor were making the decisions, on who was going to be doing the A and E work" – the architect and engineering."[76]

Presbrey also testified that he too continued to make contributions to Governor DiPrete after he reached the legal $2,000 limit by making contributions of cash. "Between checks and cash, his annual contributions went from $2,000 to $4,500, to $6,150, to more than $27,500, in DiPrete's last two years."[77]

DiPrete's co-conspirators were running for cover. One friend of Frank Zaino told the Grand Jury that he would not go to jail to protect DiPrete.

◆————————————————◆

Zaino And DiPrete
A Retrospective on Friendship

Zaino, a Charles Street native, eventually moved to Western Cranston where he met his neighbor, Edward DiPrete. "They became good friends, however, only after DiPrete was elected to serve on the Cranston School Committee. DiPrete was serving on its Building Committee when Zaino was doing work on the city's schools."[78] Zaino's career was burgeoning just as his business was growing and he was elected President of the Rhode Island Society of Professional Engineers. He "led the Society as it discussed the need to reform government-contracting rules, in the wake of scandals in Maryland involving Vice President Spiro Agnew. Ironically, Richard Nixon's Vice President had been forced to resign after pleading no-contest to taking kickbacks for state contracts when he was Governor of Maryland."[79]

Zaino's relationship with DiPrete blossomed and DiPrete's Agency provided Zaino's insurance needs while their wives became close church friends. DiPrete's eventual political rise took him from School Committee to Mayor, and Zaino's influence grew. "One Cranston architect recalled that Zaino was 'in and out of the Mayor's Office all the time.' This architect said that he relied on Zaino, his friend, to tell him where he stood on city contracts. The architect said that, to get work, Zaino had advised him: "You'll have to contribute heavily....Zaino would later tell a Grand Jury that payments made to DiPrete fundraiser Rodney Brusini were 'tied to how much work you got...in other words, if you did a lot of work, you'd better put in a lot of money."[80]

In 1984, when DiPrete ran for Governor for the first time, Zaino was his primary fundraiser, not only raising significant revenue for the cause, but also donating in excess of $20,000 himself, most of it in cash that was given directly to Brusini according to his Grand Jury testimony. Once DiPrete was elected, but even before he was inaugurated, Zaino was planning his future inquiring of outgoing Governor J. Joseph Garrahy if he knew "of any big state contracts coming up for bid."[81]

While the former Governor wasn't of much help, Zaino found his own project in the Frank Licht Judicial complex on Benefit Street in Providence. Zaino testified before the Grand Jury that he went to DiPrete friend, fundraiser and colleague, Rodney Brusini. "Brusini told Zaino," according to Grand Jury testimony, "that he would talk to Governor DiPrete about the courthouse contract." When time passed with no word, Zaino began to worry. Finally, he asked his wife, Rosemarie Zaino, to talk to Patricia DiPrete. The two had become close friends over the years. Subsequently, Zaino told the Grand Jury, he was able to get into the Governor's State House office to express his anxiety about getting the courthouse project. DiPrete promised to have his Chief of Staff track it. Later, according to Grand Jury testimony, Zaino received a phone call from Brusini: The job was his – with a catch…. Brusini asked what was 'customary' for architects and engineers to pay to get state jobs. Zaino said he'd heard the going rate was 5 percent of the fee charged for a big project, 6 percent for a smaller project. Brusini, in his Grand Jury testimony, said he promised to take it up with the Governor, and later reported to Zaino that it was a deal."[82] Because the total project fee was $1 million, Zaino's cost would be $50,000. After striking a deal to count the previous contribution of $20,000 he had made to DiPrete, he had to pay only $30,000. Zaino shared his 5-6 percent formula with other firms including Robinson Green Beretta Corp. who, after paying Brusini, was awarded the $30 million contract to build the state's new medium-security prison. Brusini later testified that he "had steered state projects to DiPrete-campaign contributors even though he had held no official position in state government."[83] But Zaino's fortunes soon started to fade.

◆————————————————◆

The Governor's Son Replaces Brusini As The "Ear To The Governor"

"It was sometime in 1988, Frank N. Zaino told the Grand Jury, that he began to sense a rift within the DiPrete camp. People were saying that Rodney Brusini, Ed DiPrete's old friend, was on the outs. Zaino saw a new face emerging;

the Governor's 28-year old son."[84] Concerned that Brusini might be "skimming," Governor DiPrete ordered Zaino to deal only with his son Dennis. The younger DiPrete later told Zaino that the payment from which they suspected Brusini of skimming was made by developer Richard Baccari on behalf of Leonard Garofalo in order for him to secure contract work for the prison intake center. Envelopes, thick with cash, flowed from Zaino to DiPrete in such large numbers that Zaino had to open a bank account in the names of his children to hide the money from his wife who had filed for divorce. "Meanwhile, Dennis DiPrete, who owned his own engineering firm, escalated his demands. In Grand Jury testimony, Zaino's son recalled Zaino's complaints: 'That's all they want – money, money, money.' "[85] The demands would continue right up until DiPrete lost his 1990 campaign to two-time challenger, millionaire Bruce Sundlun. "Even then, Dennis DiPrete wouldn't quit. In early 1991, with a new Governor in place, and most of Rhode Island embroiled in the banking crisis, he telephoned Zaino. Zaino later said that Dennis DiPrete ordered him to round up money that architects still owed for DiPrete-administration work they were doing."[86] When Zaino refused Dennis protested "they owe it to us."[87] But Zaino "said he would no longer shake people down."[88] DiPrete's world was unraveling just as President George H.W. Bush was considering him for a federal appointment. State police began to pour through Zaino's records and question his friends. Donald Conlon was indicted for perjury and Zaino believed he would talk. Zaino was offered a deal but refused when he learned he would have to plead guilty to extortion. Zaino got lucky, however, when Attorney General O'Neil agreed to an immunity deal for Zaino believing that he needed Zaino's testimony to nail Dennis DiPrete.

By fall of 1991, Zaino had told investigators how he paid Dennis DiPrete in exchange for state contracts; how Dennis had told him that he kept a log of all contributors and their contributions and how *everyone* had to pay. Investigators learned how DiPrete replaced Brusini as the person to talk to if you wanted a contract. "One contractor told a Grand Jury that he had considered Dennis DiPrete an ear to the Governor' "89

Governor Edward DiPrete in 1987.

But more, the Governor watched out for Dennis. "In 1988, *The Providence Journal* carried stories chronicling complaints from Rhode Island environmental regulators. The regulators said they'd been pressured by the Governor's office to approve wetlands permits for projects that Dennis DiPrete was working on. Officials at the Department of Environmental Management were also displeased at the state's hiring of Domenic V. Tutela, an engineer and DiPrete loyalist, to conduct an environmental study, even though his firm had been rated last among the bidders."[90] By all accounts, it was the Governor, and not his son, that secured the work for Tutela. Michael M. Doyle, DiPrete's former Chief of Staff who became one of the principals in the RDW Group, a high- powered Rhode Island based public relations firm, testified that "the Governor loved Tutela."[91]

$$\bullet \longrightarrow \bullet$$

The Governor and his Son Are Connected to The RISDIC Scandal

By all reports Governor DiPrete and his son were close. They were also the subjects of the RISDIC investigation, which, in 1992, "revealed that Edward and Dennis DiPrete had been involved in two Cranston land deals financed by questionable loans. The Commission concluded that the loans had been based on faulty appraisals, and, in one instance, on property that was largely swampland. The Commission traced a money trail from failed Rhode Island credit unions into various DiPrete bank accounts. According to state records, Paul Marchionda, Dennis DiPrete's partner from his engineering firm, and a partner in one of the ventures, testified that Dennis DiPrete had told him that the Governor was a silent partner."[92] Both DiPretes denied that the Governor was involved and said that the $30,000 check written to the Governor from Dennis was a reimbursement of Dennis's college tuition money that the Governor had paid.

Perhaps no deal the DiPretes were involved in was as spectacular as the "Cranston Land Deal." In this transaction, the DiPretes purchased land in 1988 and resold it on the same day for $2 million more than they paid, subject to a controversial zone variance that would allow for the construction of 240 apartments. Despite more than 100 residents in attendance at the zoning board hearing objecting to the project, the variance was granted. Those benefiting from the $2 million profit were the Governor and Dennis DiPrete, Dennis's brother Thomas, a son-in-law of former Cranston Mayor James Taft. "A month later, the Texas developer received a state wetlands permit to develop another piece of land in North Providence. Dennis DiPrete had done some engineering work on that property, and state environmental officials later said they had been pressured by the Governor's office to issue the permit."[93]

While publicly, the Governor issued an apology crafted by Doyle and another aid, Robert D. Murray, privately he was furious that he was forced to do so. All of this preceded the 1988 election that DiPrete won by a scant 2% of the vote.

◆————————————◆

Michael W. Piccoli Finds a Way to Expand the Governor's Fortunes

In the midst of these investigations, police were given a tip to look into a "questionable sewer-construction contract in Cranston. The investigators found themselves on the trail of Michael Piccoli, a contractor from Smithfield.

Within months, the investigators had built an overwhelming case that Piccoli had padded his construction bills in Cranston and paid kickbacks to Cranston City officials. The Investigators also found evidence that Piccoli had been wheeling and dealing at the state central landfill, which he had overseen as a DiPrete-appointed member of the board of the state Solid Waste Management Corporation. The authorities had Piccoli dead to rights. They invited him downtown for a conversation. After listening to the charges he faced, Piccoli said he would cooperate. 'I can't give you the Governor,' he said, 'but I can give you Dennis.' "[94]

Michael W. Piccoli had been trying to become part of the "DiPrete contractor store" for years. As a principal in Piccoli & Sons, a paving company, he had tried desperately to get the attention of DiPrete. He was a political contributor going back to DiPrete's mayoral days. He paved DiPrete's driveway free of charge, served as a political fundraiser and helped erect "DiPrete for Governor" signs. This kind of activity was nothing new for Piccoli. Throughout the 1980s he made millions off the City of Cranston on sewer and other projects. In exchange, he paved the driveways of city officials, and in some cases, the relatives of city officials, at no charge. Certain court documents show that Piccoli signed a contract to pave a road. While the contract required the use of 4 inches of asphalt, Piccoli used only 2 inches. To protect himself against any backlash, Piccoli provided perks to the public officials. To one he gave money to take his family to Disney World. For another, he dug the hole in his backyard so the official could have a pool installed. The court records show that he even became upset when one city official had his driveway paved by another firm. Piccoli complained that he should have been given the opportunity to perform the favor. He took Mayor Michael Trafficante to the luxury box at Fenway Park, a perk worth about $4,000. Trafficante didn't refuse. He took others golfing and still others were invited as his guest to his Florida condominium. It didn't seem to matter to Piccoli that the taxpayers of Cranston paid the bill in the form of inflated contract charges.

While "DiPrete stumped the state promising an ethical revolution in government, Piccoli & Sons labored at the candidate's house. Workers installed curbing, put in a new driveway, and resurfaced the tennis court."[95] The work took three days and despite the $7,000 to $10,000 cost indicated in court records, DiPrete paid nothing for the work.

For his loyalty to DiPrete, Piccoli's reward came in the form of an appointment to the Board of Commissioners of the State's Solid Waste Management Corporation, a quasi-public agency that owned and operated New England's largest landfill in Johnston. He also received an invitation to join the exclusive Friends of DiPrete – the Governor's campaign finance committee.

Perhaps most significantly, Piccoli had the opportunity to befriend Dennis DiPrete and the two began meeting routinely for lunch in some of the city's finest restaurants. "According to Piccoli's later testimony, Dennis DiPrete asked Piccoli to keep him informed of state work coming up at the Central Landfill; Piccoli told DiPrete of his own interest in state work. Piccoli told the Grand Jury that for state-landfill work, he had followed Dennis DiPrete's directions on selecting contractors. His testimony also revealed that he had collected contractors' contributions to Governor DiPrete's campaign."[96]

Just four years later, Attorney General O'Neil was once again in that now too familiar position of dealing with accomplices in order to get the DiPretes. In a meeting with Piccoli, O'Neil recited the bad news; "there was evidence, said O'Neil, that Piccoli had been fleecing the taxpayers for years. In Cranston, he'd stolen hundreds of thousands of dollars, submitting false bills and bribing city officials; at Solid Waste, he'd used his position to shake down contractors. Piccoli sat in silence. The only time he betrayed emotion was when O'Neil told him his wife was also in trouble, for having apparently cooked the company books. The contractor's face flushed. The attorney general brought up the state's investigation of the DiPretes and asked for Piccoli's cooperation. 'I can't give you the Governor,' responded Piccoli. 'But I can give you Dennis. Michael Piccoli pleaded guilty to taking $90,000 in bribes for state and Cranston-city contracts.' "[97]

Piccoli testified that he would let staff of the RI Solid Waste Management Corporation know if the contractor in question was the choice of Dennis DiPrete by looking out the window toward the State House and nodding. Piccoli also arranged some of his own deals with landfill contractors. "One gave him $200 a week in cash, Piccoli later told investigators, which he put in his pocket for 'walking around' money. According to court records, Piccoli told a state-police detective that he once gave the Solid Waste Chairman, Richard A. Johnson, ten $100 bills, asking Johnson to cut him in on any deals he had cooking – 'to become a player with me.' "[98] Johnson testified that despite their friendship, he refused, and cooperated with authorities. Thomas Wright, the Director of the Solid Waste Management Corporation, said "Piccoli spent an inordinate amount of time at the landfill, meddling in the day-to-day operations, as well as contract negotiations."[99]

Indeed he did! In a story typical of Rhode Island's small size and incestuous political nature, Paul Caranci, a co-author of this book, was employed by the Rhode Island Solid Waste Management Association as the organization Chief Property Manager at the same time that Piccoli was serving as its vice chairman. The primary role of the Chief Property Manager at that time was to implement the requirements of a state statute that required RISWMC to take by eminent domain all residential property located within a 1,000 foot radius of the landfill's operational boundary, and to acquire by optional purchase, all the of the residential property located between 1,000 and 2,000 feet of the landfill's operational boundary. This was a significant amount of land and was to cost the Corporation several million dollars. The controversial legislation was made necessary when the RI State Legislature, reacting to the odor and environmental complaints of landfill neighbors, many of whom purchased their properties long after the establishment of the landfill operation, passed the unfunded mandate.

In order to facilitate the mandate, Caranci drafted rules and regulations governing the program. These rules and regulations were advertised for public hearing in accordance with the provisions of the Administrative Procedures Act (APA). This lengthy process involves a public hearing, submission, acceptance and review of public comments, and a vote of approval by the Board. Once this was accomplished, the final rules and regulations were promulgated. The rules were written and approved to maintain the highest integrity in a highly visible and controversial project.

In accordance with the newly adopted rules and regulations, the RISWMC appraised the subject property using the services of certified appraisers selected through the competitive bidding process. Three were selected. Thomas Andolfo and his firm, Andolfo Appraisal Services, were contracted for the appraisal of developed residential land while William McGovern owner of Northeast Appraisal Services was selected to perform appraisals of vacant land. Bill Sweeney of Cooke & Co. Appraisal Services was contracted to act as review appraiser in the event that the Corporation's appraisal was lower than that of the property owner. The property owner, therefore, was also urged to solicit his/her own appraisal by any certified appraiser other than the ones hired by the Corporation. The caveat was that the property owner had to have his/her appraisal complete and available at the time of the initial offer. The property owner and his/her representative(s) and the RISWMC's team (consisting of Caranci, his assistant Patricia Cerbo, Arnold Johnson and Jeffrey Gladstone, the Corporation's inside and outside legal counsels respectively, and the appropriate RISWMC appraiser) would then meet so that the Corporation's offer could be disclosed. If the offer was acceptable to the property owner, the proper documents would be signed. If the property owner deemed the offer too low and had a legitimate appraisal that was higher in value, then his/her appraisal would be submitted. A review appraiser would be given the two competing appraisals and that appraiser would provide a final opinion of value. That estimate of value represented the final offer to the property owner. The final offer was binding in eminent domain cases while the property owner had the right to refuse the offer if the property were located between 1,000 and 2,000 feet of the operational boundary of the landfill. In order for the process to work fairly, it was critical that word of the value of the Corporation's appraisal be maintained in the strictest confidence. Only the aforementioned members of the "team" knew the value prior to the offer being made to the property owner. If the property owner had advanced information of the value to be offered, he/she could simply pay an unscrupulous appraiser to provide a value higher than that of the Corporation assuring that the two appraisals would be sent to review.

One of the properties being taken by eminent domain was a unique property owned by one of Piccoli's business associates. His property was unique in that in contained a grandfathered landscaping debris landfill and a tree farm. Piccoli tried relentlessly to obtain a copy of the appraisal report from the moment it was received. Despite Piccoli's threats, Caranci would not disclose the appraised value which appeared to be high due to the unique nature of the property. Finally, on a Friday afternoon, when the pressure from the Board's vice chairman became too much for Caranci to deal with, he notified RISWMC Director Thomas E. Wright of Piccoli's intimidation tactics. Wright immediately contacted Board Chairman, Richard "Dick" Johnson, who apparently called Piccoli over the weekend and told him to back off. Piccoli was compliant but upset. Piccoli marched into Caranci's office early Monday morning to let him know of his displeasure. Of course he did so in a non-descript way. "You did me a favor." Piccoli said. "Now I cannot be accused of passing the information along to the owner." As he began to walk away, he turned and said, "But I'll remember this!" Caranci had momentarily derailed Piccoli's plan, but clearly there would be a price to pay for his perceived insubordination.

While Piccoli spent his days wining and dining and golfing with government officials, his employees and partners were getting impatient. "'Where's the work?' one of his brothers would holler in the office. 'How come we're not getting any work? Not to worry, Mike assured everyone. 'A lot of gravy is coming.' "[100]

The gravy came in 1989 with the addition to the state prison's intake center. Dennis DiPrete told him "this one's yours."[101] Piccoli's firm was selected as the site's main contractor charged with overseeing all site preparation and excavation work but could not post the necessary bond required of all firms that bid on state jobs. The job went instead to Laura Donatelli, the daughter of a North Providence contractor who, as a woman, qualified as a minority contractor."[102] Because her company owned no equipment, however, she hired Piccoli as a subcontractor. Despite having crews on site seven days per week for four months and running up labor charges of $20,000 a week, Donatelli paid him only $50,000, $350,000 less than he expected. He appealed to Dennis DiPrete to force Donatelli to pony up, but he never did collect.

During this time, Piccoli met with A. Robert Lusi, another Smithfield contractor. Lusi wanted Piccoli's help in getting state jobs. Piccoli agreed to help. A few months later, Robert's brother Gus identified the state job he was interested in; the URI job, a planned $600,000 expansion of the University's Library. Both Lusis and Piccoli had a similar account of events during their Grand Jury testimony. "Piccoli told the investigators that he had reported the Lusis' interest to Dennis DiPrete. A few days later, he recalled, DiPrete told him the URI contract would cost $60,000 – 10 percent of the $600,000 fee the Lusis' stood to make. Piccoli, in his testimony, said that Gus Lusi's response to the offer was 'I'll gladly give him the $60,000.' In their testimony, the Lusi brothers said they had agreed to each put up $30,000. Robert Lusi kept his money in a safe deposit box at a Johnston branch of Fleet Bank; Gus Lusi kept his in his desk drawer....In the ensuing months, the Lusis paid $40,000 in kickbacks, including a $5,000 'finder fee' to Piccoli. The sum also included a $10,000 campaign check to 'Victory '90,' a DiPrete-sponsored Republican fundraiser featuring President George H. W. Bush ('that was an extortion in my opinion,' Gus Lusi later testified)."[103]

Piccoli testified that he extracted some revenge for Dennis DiPrete's failure to get Piccoli's money from Donatelli for the prison job. When Lusi gave Piccoli an envelope containing $15,000 meant for Dennis DiPrete, Piccoli removed $5,000 and gave only the remaining $10,000 to Dennis. But Piccoli's firm never could recover from the losses on the prison job. In the spring of 1991, *The Providence Journal* reported that Piccoli was unable to pay $9,000 in dumping fees owed to the landfill. He was forced to resign from the Corporation's Board in disgrace. In December, Piccoli & Sons closed down. Piccoli's home in Lincoln was sold and his Lincoln Continental was repossessed. He was even being trailed by a bookie for not paying several thousand dollars in gambling debts.

Financial problems notwithstanding, investigators would not let up. They were interviewing Piccoli's former employees and issued a subpoena for all his business records dealing with Cranston. As a result of the information obtained, Piccoli "pleaded guilty to five felony charges. He admitted to crimes involving the state landfill, the City of Cranston, and Governor DiPrete's administration. He was bound for prison – the only person in the DiPrete case thus far who has spent any time behind bars. A prosecutor recommended a lenient sentence, because of Piccoli's pledge to cooperate. The sentence would later become a subject of controversy when lawyers for the DiPretes noted that the prosecutors had allowed Piccoli to pay just $135,000 in restitution to the City of Cranston – far less than the $1 million he admitted stealing from the city."[104] The Lusi brothers obtained immunity as a result of their testimony about the URI payoffs.

Rodney M. Brusini Suffers Personal and Business Setbacks

In 1984, Rodney Brusini's star was on the rise. By 1990, his "personal fortunes had been in decline. In the time leading up to this January morning in 1992, Brusini had plunged into debt, separated from his wife, been rushed to the hospital for a drug overdose, and come under criminal investigation."[105] On this Monday, Brusini was meeting at Heffies Restaurant in North Kingstown with his attorney, Richard A. Gonnella, Attorney General O'Neil, and J. Richard Ratcliffe, a prosecutor in O'Neil's office, to tell them what he knew about payments for state contracts. "But Brusini would not easily surrender the secrets he purported to know. As the manager of the DiPrete insurance agency, he had earned a reputation as a shrewd businessman. He knew how to write an insurance policy."[106] Brusini told his audience that DiPrete was a control freak. To demonstrate his point, Brusini relayed the story of how DiPrete appointed him to run the State Racing and Athletics Commission in 1985. In this new position of authority, Brusini hired two men to collect urine specimens from the dogs at Lincoln Greyhound Park, for drug testing. When the Governor found out, he was furious and he had the two men fired. DiPrete then rehired them himself."[107]

Brusini was concerned about his role in the DiPrete investigation. He was willing to cooperate, but wanted to be used as a confidential source rather than a cooperating witness. He preferred not to have to testify. O'Neil wouldn't agree. Brusini then suggested a proffer – a written statement of what he would testify to. Only after receiving assurances from O'Neil that what he said wouldn't be used against him, Brusini offered his story.

Brusini and DiPrete were as close as two people could be. Friends called them "Siamese Twins." DiPrete was closer only to his wife. Both men were elected to the Cranston School Committee in 1970 and each displayed a conservative approach to education. Even when they opposed each other for the position of Chairman, the two reached a compromise that had each presiding for half the term. In 1974, each won a seat to the City Council. But, in 1978, when Mayor James Taft withdrew from the race to tend to his law practice after the sudden death of his law partner, the Republican Party selected Ed DiPrete to replace him. Brusini had retired from government service a few years earlier and was now managing the F. A. DiPrete Agency. But while he left elected office behind, "Brusini remained a force in Cranston politics. He was DiPrete's chief fundraiser."[108]

The meeting adjourned at Heffies, but continued at O'Neil's home in Narragansett. Brusini denied any involvement in the selection of architects and engineers, but "did say, according to court records, that Governor DiPrete would ask him to 'rate' certain firms competing for state contracts, in terms of how much money they had contributed to the DiPrete campaign. Often, said Brusini, the firm contributing the most would get the contract."[109] O'Neil promised to consider what Brusini told him.

Before Brusini had a chance to leave, however, O'Neil dropped a bombshell on him. O'Neil told Brusini that DiPrete had recently given O'Neil a fax meant for Brusini. The document involved Robert Haig, an architect that was just awarded a big DiPrete state contract. Brusini was more angry than surprised at the thought that DiPrete would betray him. That, more than anything else, is what persuaded Brusini to cooperate.

At a follow-up meeting, O'Neil informed Brusini that Brusini had given them no evidence that could be used against him at their first meeting, but if incriminating evidence could be gathered independently, Brusini could still be charged. O'Neil's real interest, however, seemed to be Haig and his involvement in the contract to renovate the Veterans Memorial Auditorium in 1989. "According to court records, investigators had spoken to other contractors, who had said that the DiPrete administration chose particular people to work on the Vets – including a Massachusetts engineer who'd been Dennis DiPrete's college roommate. Around the same time, Robert Haig's business records showed, the architect had given $52,000 to Brusini."[110] Brusini insisted, however, that the money was a loan from a friend, not a bribe, and that he needed it because, just having divorced his wife, he spent a lot of money on woman and trips to Florida.

O'Neil turned his attention to Frank N. Zaino, the DiPrete fundraiser and City engineer. He informed Brusini that as a cooperating witness, Zaino told them "that he had delivered money to Brusini from architects and engineers for state contracts."[111] Again, Brusini had nothing to offer.

Two weeks later, two state police auditors asked Brusini questions relating to the Rosemac Building in Providence. This was another Mollicone-owned building that was leased by the RI Department of Elderly Affairs during DiPrete's administration. They asked about Brusini's co-ownership of the building. Brusini denied being a partner. However, court records indicate that when Brusini was presented with a copy of his tax return that had been subpoenaed from Brusini's accountant, indicating that Brusini was "a half owner, Brusini appeared shaken and refused to answer any more questions. The next week, testifying before a Grand Jury,

Brusini again denied that he had been a Rosemac partner."[112] But investigators also found a letter from Brusini's accountant discussing "the tax implications of Brusini's desire to stay somewhat anonymous in the acquisition and the lease of this property. According to court records, the Attorney General's Office would later draft a list of crimes that Brusini could be charged with. The list included perjury, extortion, and racketeering."[113]

By spring of 1992, while still working at the F.A. DiPrete agency, Brusini decided to cooperate and was meeting regularly with investigators and prosecutors. The meetings were long and sometimes became contentious. Brusini often complained about how DiPrete mistreated him. Lt. Mattos would frequently call him a "bagman," a term that upset Brusini who described himself as a "fundraiser." Brusini estimated that over the years he had raised over $4 million for DiPrete, raising $1.72 million in 1984 alone. He bragged about raising $350,000 in a single fundraising event that started at DiPrete's home and ended at the Alpine Country Club.

DiPrete's campaign finance team included Michael Doyle, his chief of staff, DiPrete's legal counsel, public works director Joseph Pezza and purchasing director. Brusini sat at the helm. The group met regularly at the Mayor's conference table to review lists of contributors, taking note of those with contracts nearing expiration. Those vendors would receive extra tickets. City employees later testified to the Grand Jury that, as Mayor, DiPrete personally selected contractors on a routine basis, a practice that continued when he became

Governor. Brusini met with contributors at the F.A Di-
Prete insurance agency. "Everybody knew who Rod
was," engineer Frank Zaino told the Grand Jury, "Everybody."[114] Brusini would tell the Grand Jury that Di-
Prete wanted total control of everything that happened
in the City. And through Brusini, he had it! For example, Donald Prout, a local architect, designed the new
public library in Cranston even though DiPrete had
never asked him for a campaign contribution. "But when
Prout met with Brusini, Prout said, Brusini told him
that the Mayor wasn't pleased with the level of Prout's
campaign giving. 'We're businessmen,' Prout recalled
Brusini saying, 'and we have big, big expenses. Without
your participation, you know you're not going to be considered for work. We have to work with the people who
contribute and help us.' "[115] Prout refused and was cut
off from City work and eventually, from state work as
well. Others in the industry saw Prout as an example of
why you had to contribute to the DiPrete cause. But, for
each potential bidder that didn't play ball, there were
several more that did. "Brusini told the Grand Jury that
during DiPrete's first term as Cranston Mayor, in the
late 1970's, DiPrete instructed Brusini to meet with Anthony Capuano's company. Capuano's company held the
city's trash hauling contract. Capuano stopped by
Brusini's office and gave him an envelope with a contribution of $1,000 or $2,000 in cash, which, Brusini testified, he passed on to the Mayor. Brusini told the prosecutors that he did not include the money in DiPrete's
campaign finance report."[116] On another occasion,
Brusini, Capuano and DiPrete went to Atlantic City.
Capuano not only paid for all the rooms and meals, but

also provided a roll of money for DiPrete to use at the tables. DiPrete, who said he never took a payoff from Brusini, denies that he was given gambling money, but defended the trip saying that the contract with Capuano, which saved the City $1 million, had already been signed before they went to Atlantic City. Brusini chalked it up to the political process. Brusini also told prosecutors that he had an arrangement with DiPrete regarding cash. He "said that the Mayor told him he could keep one-third of all cash contributions – money that went unreported in campaign records – which Brusini viewed as reimbursement for his expenses."[117]

According to Brusini, DiPrete also made money from zoning variances and exceptions. He controlled the Zoning Board so "if you 'wanted to get something done in Cranston,' you had to go to Brusini, who would then meet with DiPrete. Once, Brusini told the prosecutors,

Governor DiPrete addresses a 1985 gathering at the Community College of RI.

he collected about $12,500 from one developer and took the money to the Mayor, who gave him a third of it. Another time, Brusini testified, DiPrete accused him of having failed to turn over all the money he'd collected from a developer for a zone change. According to Brusini's Grand Jury testimony, the confrontation involved $15,000 in cash that Brusini said he had delivered to DiPrete from Alfred Carpianato, a prominent local developer. The money, which Brusini testified was to secure zoning approval for an apartment complex for the elderly, had been made in two installments: $7,500 before the approval and $7,500 after. Brusini told the Grand Jury that after the second payment, DiPrete summoned him to City Hall: "He confronted me, saying that he had had a conversation with Freddy Carpianato, and he was led to believe that Carpianato had given me more money that I had actually turned over to the Mayor.' "[118] The three eventually met and the matter was resolved with nothing more being said.

Brusini and the Attorney General failed to reach an agreement and eventually, by mid-1992, the investigators stopped talking to Brusini and prepared an indictment for perjury. With the threat of indictment hanging over him, Brusini started to cooperate and talks of immunity surfaced again. "That same month, Brusini quit his job at F. A. DiPrete, where he had worked for two decades. There was no going away party."[119]

In May of 1993, prosecutors were losing their patience with Brusini. They felt Brusini was jerking them around. The prosecutors again spoke of bringing perjury charges. But before they could make up their mind, Brusini gave them an ultimatum. Either protect his financial interests in the Metcalf Building, or he would stop talking. At issue was the state's potential lease cancellation of space in the building. Prosecutors wouldn't hear of it. On May 4, 1993, Brusini was very close to indictment.

◆————————————◆

The Department of Transportation Gets a New Director

If the goal is to direct state contracts, the Department of Transportation is the place to be and DiPrete's, choice to direct that Department was Joseph Pezza. Di-Prete was advised against appointing Pezza by those closest to his organization. Pezza wasn't the most qualified person for the post. In fact, officials from the Department of Transportation (DOT) referred to him as "Joe the Dope." But the cries fell on deaf ears as DiPrete believed Pezza would be the most loyal. To help Pezza with the actual job duties, DiPrete created the position of Executive Director and appointed Senator John Chafee's cousin, businessman Duncan H. Doolittle, to the post.

"Pezza made his agenda clear at his first staff meeting. According to Grand Jury testimony from Patrick J. Quinlan, who was the DOT's chief legal counsel at the time, Pezza stunned the assembled DOT officials: 'You guys have been running this place for quite a while. Now it's our turn.' Asked about this statement in an interview held some years later, Pezza responded: 'I never remember that. Definitely not.' As the head of the trans-

portation department, Pezza sidestepped the formal con-
tract-selection process, telling his subordinates to hire
the contractors whom he designated. The officials ob-
jected. Doolittle confronted Pezza, shouting, 'You're going to jail,' " Quinlan told the grand jury.[120]

None of this rattled Pezza. He knew he had the
support of the Governor and was therefore able to over-
rule them. According to Quinlan, Pezza and two partners
of a New York firm that had won the multi-million dollar
bid to construct the Jamestown – Verrazzano Bridge, had
lunch on the second floor of Camille's Roman Garden, a
classic restaurant in the heart of Providence's Federal
Hill neighborhood, to celebrate the signing of a contract
that had just taken place in the Governor's office. After
lunch, while walking down the stairs, "Pezza asked the
contractors for campaign contributions. The contractors
expressed surprise. Quinlan, the DOT legal counsel, testified that shortly after the luncheon he received a phone
call from the contractor's lawyer, in New York. The lawyer told Quinlan that the contractors didn't want to start
out on the wrong foot, but that they felt uncomfortable
about Pezza's request. Quinlan testified that he told the
lawyer that it was a common practice in Rhode Island but
that the New York firm had won the contract and
shouldn't feel obligated. Nevertheless, the contractors ultimately gave to the DiPrete campaign."[121]

Pezza turned to Brusini every time the Department hired a contractor for any purpose. In so doing, he
shunned the DOT experts. "Brusini would later tell investigators that he considered only their political contributions, not their professional qualifications. Pezza, said

Brusini, 'knew the drill' from their Cranston days."[122] According to the testimony of both Brusini and Pezza, since his days working at City Hall, Pezza would bring a list of bidders on contracting jobs to the F.A. DiPrete agency to ask for Brusini's guidance. "Brusini took the list of bidders to the State House, where, he testified, he would brief DiPrete on how much money each contractor had given. DiPrete would go down the list, making check marks beside certain names, said Brusini. Then Brusini would deliver the list with the Governor's choices back to Pezza."[123]

Michael Doyle, Governor DiPrete's Chief of Staff, was surprised that even as Governor, DiPrete wanted to approve *every* contract, even those under $20,000. "I still want everything to come up to me,"[124] DiPrete said. "Doyle told the investigators that Brusini met regularly with the Governor to update him on campaign contributors, and then DiPrete would tell his aides whom to choose for a project. The Governor's favorite expression when designating his choices, as recalled by Doyle and several other aides, was 'all things being equal.' "[125] DiPrete felt that his selections were not only good policy, but good politics as well. According to Doyle, he would frequently say, "you can delegate duties, but not responsibility."[126]

But Pezza was becoming a political liability according to Duncan Doolittle who called him "the most incompetent man I've ever met, and stupid as well."[127] During his tenure at DOT, there were a number of "scandals involving his management and his hiring of contractors. Doolittle, who had publicly criticized Pezza, was consigned to a basement office in the State House, and then resigned. Pezza resigned eight months after he had begun. Some DOT staffers had T-shirts made up, proclaiming, 'I survived Joe the Dope.' "[128]

While Pezza was forced to resign because of the DOT scandals, DiPrete's popularity with the voters remained high. The Governor survived the scandals, but Brusini did not. With the embarrassment of the investigation into DOT, DiPrete publicly "expressed dismay, and questioned the propriety of Brusini's having communicated with Joseph Pezza."[129] Brusini was told by another DiPrete aide that he had to "take the heat for the Governor. After DiPrete's 1986 reelection, Brusini resigned as campaign-finance chairman, saying he was burned out. He later told investigators that Governor DiPrete had hung him 'out to dry' "[130]He was certainly bitter. He had been DiPrete's leading fundraiser since DiPrete started his political career. After acting like DiPrete's brother, he was now being pushed aside in favor of the Governor's son, and Dennis had made it clear that he didn't trust Brusini. The Governor had already informed Zaino, another DiPrete fundraiser, that he thought Brusini was skimming. "From now on, the Governor told Zaino, deal with Dennis."[131]

◆————————————————◆

Sullivan, Mollicone and Brusini — Again!

Governor DiPrete would describe his problem with Brusini as "a 'periodic cooling' between old friends"[132]. Although Brusini continued his service on the campaign committee, he would liken his situation to having "political aids."[133] But according to Brusini's testimony to the Grand Jury, his old partner, Joe Mollicone, and the Governor's mistress would help him patch up his relationship with the Governor.

In 1985, Brusini, who was then DiPrete's Finance Chairman, Mollicone and Joseph M. Cerilli, purchased "and renovated the old *Providence Journal* Building, a beautiful turn of the century structure in the heart of Downtown Providence, and were trying to rent space to the state. Cerilli later told the Grand Jury that he had approached a friend, H. James Field, Jr., the chairman of DiPrete's political organization. Field, a successful businessman, had been a White House aide to President Gerald R. Ford and was a former chairman of the Rhode Island Republican Party. Cerilli testified that he had promised Field 'a substantial contribution' to secure a lease with the state. Field promised to check it out, Cerilli testified, and later Field reported that 'we can help you' – for 'a substantial contribution. One day, according to court records, Brusini said that Field pulled him aside after a State House meeting and advised him that the Rhode Island Housing and Mortgage Finance Corporation would be moving into the old *Providence Journal* building. Field told Brusini to collect $25,000 from Mollicone and Cerilli 'in green,' Brusini told investigators."[134] Brusini had lunch with Mollicone and Cerilli at Capricios, a restaurant in Providence, and was given envelopes containing between $12,000 and $14,000 [135], which he gave to DiPrete. At a second meeting a week later, Brusini accepted more cash laden envelopes and gave those to DiPrete as well. (In 1993, Field defended his actions saying he did nothing wrong and would cooperate with the investigators. But during Grand Jury questioning months later, Field pleaded the 5th refusing to incriminate himself.)

Brusini was making DiPrete a lot of money, but he was always taken care of in the process. "According to court records, a contractor seeking state work landscaped the yard of Brusini's water-view house in Jamestown at no charge; another contractor built him a deck. Brusini also became a 'consultant' to Wall Street underwriters seeking lucrative Rhode Island bond work. One paid him $2,000 a month, according to court records, another paid him $1,500 a month, even though, Brusini testified, 'I was not an expert in the field.' " An executive at Bear, Stearns, a Wall Street investment underwriter, offered to raise $20,000 to $25,000 for DiPrete in exchange for getting a "foothold" in the state. After getting DiPrete's permission, Bear, Stearns hired Brusini as a $2,000 per month consultant to keep them apprised of upcoming Rhode Island bond issues. Bear, Stearns denied any involvement and wrongdoing.

◆————————————————◆

The Brusini And Mollicone Relationship Flourishes, And, Thanks To The Governor, So Does Brusini's Bank Account

Brusini and Mollicone became friends and spent a lot of "leisure time" together. In 1990 Brusini reported an income of $175,000 with a net worth of $1.4 million. Still, he needed to borrow $500,000 from friends and relatives to keep his empire going. Mollicone started to partner with

Brusini and Brusini secured state tenants for two of their buildings. "In 1988, Mollicone told Brusini that he was interested in buying the Rosemac Building, at 160 Pine Street and asked him to check with the Governor about getting a state tenant. Brusini became a silent partner, court documents show; according to Mollicone, Brusini wanted his involvement concealed until the lease was 'signed, sealed and delivered.' "[136] When Brusini asked DiPrete for a state tenant, DiPrete told him it would cost $20,000. Shortly thereafter the Department of Elderly Affairs moved into the building and Brusini delivered $10,000 cash to DiPrete. He never asked for the balance. Mollicone then asked Brusini to join with him in the purchase of the Metcalf Building, an ambitious venture; "a grand scheme,"[137] according to Brusini. Partners in Pine Street Realty Trust, the owner of the Metcalf Building, included Robert Weisberg, a Fleet Bank executive to help secure financing, attorney Matt Marcello, a partner in Hinckly Allen Snyder & Comen, to do the legal work, Henry Fazzano, a well connected businessman, successful businessmen Edward Ricci, Joseph DiBattista, and ...Rodney Brusini, because he could secure the building's state tenant. Mollicone suggested the Department of Employment Security because he heard they were looking for new space. "'I won't stand in your way' Brusini recalled the Governor saying – provided the bid was competitive. Brusini said he pointed out to the Governor that the Pine Street Realty partners would be supportive of DiPrete's reelection campaign. 'How supportive?' DiPrete asked, according to Brusini's testimony."[138] Brusini promised that each partner could contribute between $5,000 and $7,000, well in excess of the $2,000 legal limit. Ultimately, the Pine Street Partners contributed about $30,000 to DiPrete, apparently enough, because the Department of Employment Security became the new tenant of the Metcalf Building.

While Brusini enjoyed a lavish lifestyle, collecting cars, joining exclusive clubs, and dining at expensive restaurants, he frequently had to borrow money. Mollicone lent him money to pay his Pine Street partnership expenses, and pay his son's Cornell University tuition. Mollicone wondered if he was skimming from the cash that Mollicone was providing to pay DiPrete for the state leases telling the Grand Jury that he never fully trusted Brusini.

"After Rodney Brusini's resignation, in 1986, as DiPrete's finance chairman, it was more than money that brought him back into the Governor's good graces, Brusini told investigators. Brusini testified that in the final years of the DiPrete administration – 1989 and 1990 – he helped the Governor carry on an extra-marital affair with one of DiPrete's aides, Sandra C. Sullivan. After meeting the assistant Citizens Bank branch manager when DiPrete was Mayor of Cranston, he hired her for a high-level job at the state housing agency once he became Governor. After DiPrete gave her resume to the agency director, she became the only candidate to be interviewed for the position. Quiet at first, Sullivan's position became the subject of controversy after "DiPrete's Chief of Staff, Robert D. Murray, was indicted for having obtained an improper state mortgage. Sullivan had handled Murray's loan application at Citizens. Murray was ultimately acquitted after Sullivan testified that she had made a mistake on the application. The Governor stood by Sullivan in the face of criticism by his political opponents. Her hiring, he said, reflected his desire to encourage employment of more women in state government. In 1988 Sullivan moved to the Governor's staff, and the next year she was promoted to Deputy Chief of Staff, with a salary of $57,000 a year. From her office, adjacent to the Governor's, she managed his schedule and the politically sensitive task of distributing low-number license plates, a coveted commodity in Rhode Island. Brusini testified that Sullivan also reviewed, with the Governor, campaign contributions from state vendors. Sometime after she came to work for the Governor, Brusini testified, Sullivan and DiPrete – both married – became romantically involved."[139] While Sullivan denied having an affair with Di-Prete, two others, one a DiPrete fundraiser and the other a Sullivan friend, confirmed it according to *The Providence Journal.*

Their meetings were discrete and often took place at out-of-state hotels. Initially, Roger Messier, a DiPrete friend and fundraiser, would make the hotel arrangements. But as the frequency grew, DiPrete called Brusini. Among their favorite spots were the Days Inn in Mansfield, MA, the Boston Harbor Hotel or the Boston Marriott-Long Wharf, both waterfront hotels, or the Providence Marriott. "Brusini would drive to the designated hotel ahead of time, he testified, and register in his name; then he would pick up the Governor and drive him there. DiPrete would call Sullivan from the State House or from the car, Brusini told the Grand Jury, and tell her where to meet him. Usually, Brusini would walk through the lobby with DiPrete, in case DiPrete was recognized, it might seem strange, said Brusini, for the Governor to be floating around a hotel by himself. In the spring of 1989, DiPrete appointed Brusini to the state Board of Elections, a patronage prize that paid

$36,000 a year and carried a 14-year term. Brusini would later tell prosecutors that the job was a reward – for his fundraising efforts and for his assistance with Sandra Sullivan."[140]

In his Grand Jury testimony, Brusini described one Saturday that really stood out in his mind. As he was driving the Governor back to Cranston from the Mansfield, MA hotel, he handed the Governor an envelope with $10,000 cash, a payment from Mollicone for the Department of Elderly Affairs lease at the Rosemac Building. He then dropped the Governor off at the F.A. DiPrete agency in Cranston. "A few days later, Brusini testified, when he saw DiPrete at the State House, the Governor recounted what had happened next: DiPrete had gone to Walt's Roast Beef, next door to the DiPrete agency, and bought a sandwich; then he sat in his car and ate it. Driving home, he couldn't find the envelope and realized he had thrown the $10,000 away. He hurried back to Walt's and rummaged through the trash to find it. 'He thought it was a pretty funny story,' Brusini told the Grand Jury. 'And I said, well, easy come, easy go, I guess' "[141]

The Lavish Worlds of DiPrete and Brusini Begin To Crumble

Both Brusini and DiPrete would see their world crumble at the start of the new decade. Mollicone's embezzlement of $13 million had initiated the banking crisis. The

combination of that plus the ongoing investigation under-
mined Brusini's investments especially his partnership
holdings with the now missing Mollicone.

The weak economy and ethical questions involving
his administration also hurt DiPrete. *The Providence Journal* had just run a damaging series on political favoritism
at the Public Building Authority that began a shakeup of
that organization.

By 1991, Brusini was divorced, had an enormous
debt and was facing civil suits and a criminal investigation.
He was also courting an employee of the Board of Elections
where he held a position on the Board. His problems were
overwhelming. One day early that year, Brusini's friend,
Henry Fazzano, found Brusini lying on his bed. He had apparently taken pills and alcohol and needed to be rushed to
the hospital. Brusini denies having attempted suicide, but
Fazzano wasn't convinced.

By late 1991, as DiPrete began to hear whispers of
the state's investigation, he went to see Attorney General
O'Neil in his office. "The Attorney General asked the former Governor how he would feel if Rodney Brusini were
sitting in O'Neil's office the next week. DiPrete replied, "I
have nothing to worry about from Rod Brusini."[142]

Originally wanting to charge Brusini because of his
lack of cooperation, by "the fall of '93, the prosecutors' sen-
timent had changed. J. Richard Ratcliffe, who had worked
on the case since the beginning, argued that the state
needed Brusini's testimony in order to indict DiPrete; if the
prosecutors charge Brusini, they risk losing him as a witness. Besides, it could take two years to bring Brusini to
trial, a delay that could jeopardize the DiPrete case."[143]
James W. Ryan, Chief of the Criminal Division, believed

the DiPrete case was strong "because much of the money
in question was easily traceable. The case, he said, was like
a mosaic. There was a pattern of corruption dating back to
DiPrete's days in Cranston. Contractors had admitted
making payoffs; they had gotten state work and the Governor had exercised tight control over the selection of state
contractors, according to the testimony of Brusini and
other witnesses. Brusini, for all his baggage, had been by
DiPrete's side for years. The cumulative weight of the evidence, Ryan suggested, would be enough to get a jury 'over
the bridge. On February 3, 1994 – shortly before Rodney
Brusini received immunity and went before the Grand Jury
that would be only the second to indict a former Rhode Island Governor, Ryan met with Brusini' "[144] He emphasized
the importance of telling everything he knew and not doing
anything that would destroy his credibility as a witness. In
March of 1994, DiPrete found himself waiting with his
youngest son in a Providence law office, for word on
whether the Grand Jury would indict him.

A Former Governor Goes on Trial, The First Since Thomas Wilson Dorr

Edward DiPrete laughed when his friend told him
he was about to be indicted. Rumors had been circulating
in political circles for a long time. DiPrete had heard them,
but no action was ever taken. This day would be different.
As DiPrete drove away from his luncheon, he received a
call from his attorney. "The Attorney General's office had

called: The Grand Jury was voting on his indictment to-
morrow.

The next morning, March 29, 1994, 18 men and
women filed into a grand jury room in the Kent County
Court House.[145] It took the Grand Jury less than 4 hours to
bring back 24 counts of racketeering, bribery, perjury and
extortion against DiPrete and his son Dennis. On April 13,
1994, the two pleaded not guilty at their Superior Court
arraignment. "Later that day, at state-police headquarters,
in Scituate, the DiPretes were fingerprinted and photo-
graphed in the same dingy room used to process accused
drug dealers and murderers.

The lines were quickly drawn between the accused
and the accuser."[146] Jeffrey Pine, the new Attorney General, said that the indictments and the subsequent trial of
a public figure would erase years of public corruption and
restore accountability in the system. DiPrete's attorney,
Richard M. Egbert, for his part, said the government was
relying on witnesses that were "convicted felons, disgrun-
tled employees, people who have sold their souls."[147] Egbert
was an experienced criminal defense lawyer, whose client
list included Chief Justice Joseph A. Bevilacqua, mobsters
Frank Selemme, Bobo Marrapese, Bobby Deluca, Gerard
Ouimette and a host of doctors, lawyers, politicians and
bank presidents. His expertise and success rate warranted
a fee of $400.00 per hour. "'I don't care how many guilty go
free,' said Egbert 'as long as the system is working right.' -
even 'the worst bum in the world is entitled to be prosecuted fairly and honestly.' "[148]

Dennis DiPrete hired Robert Popeo, another Boston
lawyer. The firm he helped build represented corporate gi-

ants such as Arthur Anderson, the international account-
ing firm that would be the subject of its own corporate scandal in the late 1990's, and America Online. Popeo specialized in representing those accused of white-collar crimes.
"A former federal prosecutor and magistrate, Popeo understood the legal system from all angles, and was considered
a brilliant tactician."[149] Even so, after examining the evidence against his client, "he didn't like the odds. The
case against the DiPretes encompassed 20 years of
wrongdoing. There were 75 witnesses, hundreds of
hours of Grand Jury tapes, and close to a million pages
of documents – enough to fill 600 cardboard boxes."[150]
Popeo worried that the presumption of innocence would
be lost, that the evidence would make it appear that "under Governor DiPrete, the entire state had been for sale.
Popeo's own surveys of potential Rhode Island jurors
found a climate poisonous to the DiPretes."[151]

Popio and Egbert considered the options; plead
not guilty, nolo or plea bargain, that is plead guilty in
exchange for a lighter sentence. But DiPrete maintained
his innocence. Popio explained to Dennis just how bad
things looked. "'Get real,' he'd say 'look what you're up
against.' 'I'm not your priest,' he said, 'I'm your lawyer.'
"[152] But there was just no convincing the DiPretes.

At one point, in December of 1985, with the trial
just months away, Dennis started to weaken. He spoke
to his father about the possibility of a deal. But the former Governor wouldn't hear of it. "Dennis...there's no
way I'm going to admit to something I didn't do."[153] The
two argued about the issue again at a family function,
but Edward DiPrete wouldn't budge. The walls were
crashing in and former Governor DiPrete was feeling

the pressure. The Ethics Commission fined him $30,000 for steering contracts to his political friends. He was fighting the public's perception that he caused the banking crisis. He lost his bid for re-election, was forced to go back to work at his insurance agency, and was feeling the sting of what he perceived as a betrayal by his former, loyal friend and fundraiser Rodney Brusini. He began gambling at Foxwoods Casino in Connecticut. He would listen to Brusini's Grand Jury tapes and dispute each of his lies. To prove his point, he took a lie detector test and passed, but the result, as is the case in most states, was not admissible in court.

By May of 1996, the defense team had already cost the DiPretes $1 million. Egbert and Popeo disagreed on what the defense should focus on. Popeo focused on the 600 boxes of paper evidence, while Egbert felt the case would be made by examining the witnesses' greed, lies, hidden motives and deals. The one thing they agreed on was that they would be able to exploit flaws in the state's case. Now, all they needed to do was find them.

◆────────────────────◆

Attorney General Jeffrey B. Pine Assembles The State's Prosecution Team

During his 1992 campaign against James O'Neil for attorney general, 37-year old Jeffrey Pine was hard on O'Neil for being soft on crime. "Rhode Island's image as a corrupt state would not change, said Pine, 'until we remove those who are responsible' along with those 'who haven't done enough, or who haven't done their job.' "[154] As the race between O'Neil and Pine got close, it also got dirty. Pine attacked O'Neil for a "political" indictment of Cranston Mayor Michael Trafficante for soliciting campaign contributions from City vendors – a case that grew out of the case against DiPrete. Pine questioned the timing of the indictment being issued just one month before an election.

Just after the inauguration, prosecutor Richard Ratcliffe sent Pine a confidential 27-page memo detailing the case against the DiPretes. He felt the case against Dennis was stronger than that against his father because of the testimony of Piccoli and Zaino. Most prosecutors within the attorney general's office, however, felt the high profile case was too complicated; too overwhelming for an office the size of this one to handle. "Several prosecutors said that the DiPrete investigation had gotten out of control – like an underground fire, said one, consuming precious time and resources. Another lawyer called the case 'a labyrinth of detail, but not a lot of credible people.' Indeed, Ratcliffe, in the memo to Attorney General Pine, wrote that the investigators suspected their potential star witness, Rodney Brusini, of having lied about a $52,000 loan from a state contractor."[155]

◆————————————◆

Michael F. Burns Is Rehired
To Lead the DiPrete Investigation

To lead the case, Pine rehired Michael F. Burns. Burns, "a bold young prosecutor who loved taking on the really bad guys," was fired and banished from the Attorney

General's office by O'Neil in 1989 after O'Neil questioned Burn's judgment. Burns was quick to support Pine's election campaign and it now looked as if he might be appointed to head the AG's Criminal Division. After graduating New England School of Law in 1983, Burns went to work as a "prosecutor and rose quickly through the ranks. He developed a command of the rules of evidence, an ability to think on his feet, and a dogged style in breaking down evasive witnesses. Commenting on Burns' tenacity with witnesses, a judge once remarked that only his wife could carry on an argument longer than Burns.

Within a few years Burns had moved into a showcase job in the Attorney General's office, prosecuting organized crime cases. In 1987, at the age of 29, he scored one of his biggest triumphs, a murder conviction of Bobo Marrapese. Relying on confessed criminals as witnesses and going up against the prominent Boston defense lawyer Richard Egbert, Burns persuaded a jury to convict Marrapese of a murder that had taken place 12 years earlier."[156]

That same year, Burns also led the Peter Gilbert case in which a plea bargain was struck that allowed Gilbert to be held in the custody of Providence Police for the full term of his ten-year sentence in exchange for his testimony that could have led to the indictments of several mobsters, including New England crime boss Raymond Patriarca. But Gilbert was treated more as a friend of the police than their prisoner. The state spent a total of $160,000 on Gilbert's incarceration. Expenses included the refurbishing of his police-station apartment, eight trips to Florida to see family, liquor, drugs, jewelry and cars. "It all came apart in June 1988, when Gilbert, at age 43, died of a heart attack after a traffic altercation. He was alone, driving to Connecticut to go skydiving, with 19 packets of cocaine in his parachute bag."[157] The investigation, conducted by a special mayoral commission, determined that the state "had been bamboozled by Gilbert, 'an artful manipulator, skilled in the deception of his fellow man. It appears,' the report concluded, 'that Gilbert received far greater benefits from his bargain than did the State of Rhode Island.' "[158] In 1989, Burns resigned from the office of the Attorney General saying he felt that he became the scapegoat for the Gilbert affair.

Jeff Pine accused his political opponent, Jim O'Neil of being soft on crime. Pine himself would later be questioned about the light sentence imposed on the DiPretes as a result of a plea agreement with Pine's office, (1993 photo)

During the time that Burns was in private practice, he was retained to represent a former DiPrete aide who was being questioned as part of the "jobs for sale" scheme during the DiPrete administration. Investigators spoke to the aide briefly in 1992; it appeared they were more interested in scaring him. In 1993, he was questioned again, but denied any quid-pro-quo in the jobs that he awarded, despite having solicited some of them for donations to the DiPrete campaign. He was never questioned again.

Prosecutor Steven Murray sent a memo to Pine disclosing the potential conflict. He didn't want anything to discredit the case against DiPrete. While Richard Ratcliffe had envisioned himself as taking the lead in the DiPrete case, Judge Robert D. Krause seemed to dash those hopes when he berated Ratcliffe and the state's case against Laura Donatelli who had been charged with obtaining money under false pretenses in her dealings with Michael Piccoli. Krause indicated that he felt the state brought the case against Donatelli as a means of getting her cooperation in the DiPrete case. Donatelli was acquitted after a three-day trial, but later pled guilty to a related charge of filing a false document.

◆————————————————◆

DiPrete Co-Prosecutor Joseph DeCaporale Carries Some Baggage of His Own

Pine asked another member of his team to help out on the DiPrete case. Joseph L. DeCaporale, Jr., according to Pine, brought a wealth of knowledge to the case. What

Pine didn't know is that he also brought to the case a private censure by the Rhode Island Supreme Court for professional misconduct.

In 1992, DeCaporale became a prosecutor in Attorney General O'Neil's office. He had hoped to become a judge one day. He was forty-eight years old, and looking to begin life anew. Life had thrown him many curve balls. He worked his way back from "two bankruptcies, a divorce, hospitalization for 'major depression,' and complaints from clients."[159] Now, just as he was about to help prosecute the DiPrete case, he learned that the Supreme Court was scheduling confidential hearings regarding a complaint that DeCaporale had stolen money from a former client. "DeCaporale had signed the client's name on a $21,000 check received in settlement of a police-brutality lawsuit, and kept the money. DeCaporale said he had endorsed the check and kept the money, as his legal fee, with the client's permission."[160] So, instead of beginning a new, high profile, criminal case, DeCaporale was suspended without pay by O'Neil.

Despite complaining that he could never make any money practicing law, he loved the courtroom. In court, he was the "voice of righteousness and indignation – seeking to generate sympathy for his client, pointing the finger at the accuser, the police, and the prosecutors. He had a presence, said one lawyer, a knack for understanding what was important to a jury."[161]

DeCaporale learned from the best. After graduating law school, he worked with John F. Cicilline, the father of future Providence Mayor and RI Congressman David Cicillini, and Joseph A. Bevilacqua, a future Supreme Court Chief Justice, "in a thriving criminal-defense practice that featured an array of mobster-clients, including the New England Mafia boss, Raymond L. S. Patriarca."[162] He also worked part-time as a lawyer for the Legislature and as a public defender, a position that he eventually took on full-time. When money got tight, he left his $23,000 position with the state and re-entered private practice with Cicilline and Bevilacqua.

In February of 1971, DeCaporale and another lawyer were accused of embezzling at least $4,000 from a receivership they had been involved with. Judge Ronald R. Lagueux called the two lawyers "interlopers." DeCaporale denied receiving any money and blamed the other lawyer for the problem. In a settlement, however, "DeCaporale and the other lawyer agreed to repay $4,000 to the receivership, to settle a lawsuit they said would have cost them more to defend."[163]

While with Cicilline he took part in the defense of high profile organized crime figures. Cicilline, meanwhile, was getting close to the clients he was defending. He said it was necessary to "socialize with 'these people,' referencing his mobster clients. But these relationships were beginning to draw the attention of law enforcement. In 1978 Cicilline hired as a paralegal Mafia underboss Nicholas Bianco, freshly paroled from federal prison. The next year, Cicilline, who had split from Bevilacqua, opened an office with DeCaporale on Federal Hill's Atwells Avenue. Later, a few other lawyers joined them."[164] Cicilline rented space in a building owned by crime boss Raymond L. S. Patriarca, whose vending machine business was located right across the street. On the wall hung photos of Patriarca and his son, the man who would take over as boss of the crime family upon his father's death. He and DeCaporale would routinely go for drinks with their mob clients.

All this activity gave reason for the FBI to plant bugs in the law office as part of their case against Patriarca and Bianco. While there was nothing damaging on the tapes regarding DeCaporale, the incident created enough anxiety for him to leave Cicilline and focus his practice on civil work from a new East Side office.

By 1988, following his divorce, bankruptcy and legal problems, he decided to quit the practice of law and become an insurance agent. DeCaporale wrote insurance policies and was fairly good at it. One year, he actually won a trip for two to Puerto Rico because he reached his sales quota. But he just wasn't happy outside the courtroom and he eventually returned to the practice with the Public Defenders Office.

In 1992, DeCaporale, the man who defended and befriended mobsters, finally landed a job in the Attorney General's office as a prosecutor. "Attorney General O'Neil, who had previously been unwilling to put DeCaporale in charge of organized-crime cases, hired him because he needed an experienced trial lawyer to help clear a backlog of cases."[165] The move from criminal defense lawyer to public defender to state prosecutor may be unusual, but for DeCaporale it meant more money and a good possibility for advancement. The celebration lasted only one month before O'Neil suspended him when O'Neil learned of the disciplinary charges against him.

The latest charges represented the second time in fifteen years that he was before the disciplinary board. He pled his case and his attorney, Stephen Famiglietti, suggested that the disciplinary board give DeCaporale the benefit of the doubt because "his entire career is hanging in the balance..."[166]After conferring with Famiglietti, who said that DeCaporale would probably not be disbarred or suspended from the practice of law, O'Neil decided to allow DeCaporale to work as a prosecutor while he awaited his fate. After the election in which Pine defeated O'Neil, a mutual friend put in a good word with Pine and DeCaporale was assigned to Special Prosecutions. Later in 1993, a three-member panel of lawyers recommended that the complaint against DeCaporale be dismissed. The full Board, however, disagreed and felt that some type of disciplinary action was in order. The outcome of the case now rested with the RI Supreme Court. In December, "DeCaporale pleaded for mercy before the state's five highest judges. Tearfully, DeCaporale said that he should have acted differently. What he did, he said, was a mistake, an isolated occurrence. He said that he should have gotten his client's permission in writing, or driven to Burrillville to get the client's signature. Ultimately, there were no public sanctions, but the Court did issue a private censure. While the client never collected any money, the client's brother – another former client – sued DeCaporale for misappropriating money in other instances. DeCaporale agreed to pay $17,500 over a five-year period so that the case would not result in a trial that might jeopardize his career.

◆————————————————————◆

Pine's Staff Reorganization
Puts The DiPrete Case In Jeopardy

DeCaporale was assigned to the DiPrete case, but at least one member of the prosecution's team wasn't pleased. Ratcliffe felt, that after four years of working on the case, he was being pushed out. This was not Pine's only move. In a reorganization that surprised most of the 100 member staff, Pine removed James Ryan as head of the criminal division and replaced him with Michael Burns. DeCaporale was promoted to head of Special Prosecutions to replace Burns. In May of 1995, not wanting to deal with the internal office politics, Richard Ratcliffe resigned his position as a prosecutor, one that he had held for seven years. "In retrospect, some members of the Attorney General's office saw the moment as a critical event in the history of the DiPrete case. Ratcliffe's resignation, they said, took 'the detail guy' out of the equation: the one prosecutor who had been there from the beginning, the person who knew the complex case best."[167]

◆————————————————————◆

Judge Domenic Cresto
And Pre-Trial Shenanigans

It was now August 24, 1995, and Judge Cresto was listening to pre-trial motions from the seven lawyers who

were preparing to either defend or prosecute the Di-
Pretes. Defense lawyers were requesting, in addition to
the 600 boxes of documents and 200 volumes of Grand
Jury testimony, all exculpatory evidence – "the evidence
of any crimes committed by the state's witnesses, and
any contradictory statements that might have been made
to the authorities that would cast doubt on the witnesses'
testimony. The DiPrete lawyers also wanted to know of
any 'promises, rewards, or inducements' that prosecutors
had offered their star witnesses."[168] In Rhode Island,
prosecutors are required to supply this type of information to the defense in order to ensure a fair trial. Robert Popeo believed that the state had not turned over all
their information. Popeo, giving the state the benefit of
the doubt, chalked it up to sloppiness on the part of the
state. Bruce Astrachan, the man who filled Ratcliffe's
spot on the prosecution team, responded, the defense
lawyers "'have the testimony of all the conspirators. They
have all the documents relied on in the testimony, and
there should be no surprise to them as to what may come
out at trial, Your Honor."[169] He continued, "I'm not sure
what the court could order the state to deliver to them,
in that they have everything."[170] Popeo protested that by
giving the defense 600 boxes of evidence, there was no
way they could find the document they needed. "'If the
government knows where it is,' said Popeo, 'they should
tell us, not play games.' "[171]

Joseph DeCaporale insisted the information had
been provided and the state shouldn't have to do the defense lawyer's work. But Judge Cresto disagreed. He "determined it should not be left to the DiPrete lawyers to
go through every scrap of the state's evidence for relevant

information; he assigned the prosecutors the task of extracting the needles from the haystack."[172] Astrachan argued that statements taken from witnesses by a prosecutor would be considered "work product." notes and memos reflecting legal strategies, and to those, the defense is not entitled. Cresto in response ordered the files turned over to him so the judge, not the prosecution team, would decide what the defense could have. DeCaporale was unmoved. He believed that the defense motion was posturing.

Astrachan was a new member of the DiPrete prosecution team and had only been working as a prosecutor for a year. So, despite signing his name to numerous documents indicating that the DiPrete team had everything, he was really relying on the words of Joseph DeCaporale and Michael Burns. It wasn't until sometime after the pre-trial hearing in August of 1995, about 3 months after being assigned to the case, that Astrachan learned otherwise. That's when he, Burns and DeCaporale met in a conference room of the state-police Financial Crimes unit, the "warehouse" for the DiPrete documents. "Gina Merandi, a state police employee in charge of the records, would later testify that she had hauled in 10 cardboard boxes for the three prosecutors to review. The boxes contained the work files of the original DiPrete investigators. The three men spent almost the entire day reviewing the boxes and taking out those documents they believed they would have to give to Judge Cresto. Burns later testified that he didn't stay that long and that he allowed DeCaporale and Astrachan to do most of the work. But Merandi recalled that the men reviewed information damaging to Rodney Brusini, the state's star witness. "The information could be dynamite in the hands of the DiPrete lawyers, enabling them to attack inconsistencies in Brusini's story and to argue that he had agreed to testify against Edward DiPrete to avoid a perjury charge...When they had finished, many documents remained that would not be turned over. Among them were files concerning Brusini – including information bearing on whether he had committed perjury."[173]

Burns was the man assigned to question Brusini. He should have been aware of every document that related to his witness. But he had other things on his mind. His new position was very demanding and pulled him in several different directions at the same time. He was going through a very messy and public divorce with Patricia Nugent Burns, his wife and office aide. Patricia, in a drunkard state on May 18, 1995 called 911 and reported an assault on her by Burns. Johnston police eventually dropped the case, but the tape of the 911 call was played on a local TV station, something that proved very embarrassing for Burns.

While Burns was responsible for questioning Brusini, it was DeCaporale who had the responsibility of complying with Judge Cresto's order to turn over all evidence to him or the DiPrete lawyers. Egbert was right to be suspicious. DeCaporale had a history of withholding evidence in trials. In a case involving real estate developer James Procaccianti and his uncle, a case in which they were charged with defrauding the former Marquette Credit Union of $500,000 in loan money, he failed to turn over evidence that significantly weakened the case against Procaccianti. The charges were eventually dismissed when the case went to trial. Egbert suspected that the state was withholding something about the only man who had testified that he delivered kickbacks directly to the Governor – Rodney Brusini. "Through private investigators' digging into Brusini's business dealings, Egbert concluded that Brusini had pocketed the alleged kickback money; then, with the police closing in, Brusini had implicated DiPrete to save himself."[174] The state had turned over documents regarding Brusini's statements from 1992 and 1994, but he had received nothing from the year 1993. Egbert wondered if Brusini made statements that year that might be helpful to the defense. Dennis DiPrete's lawyer was also checking into the background of Frank Zaino, the chief witness against his client. Popeo, like Egbert, would argue that Zaino kept the money he had claimed to have given Dennis DiPrete. Popeo was interested in the lavish lifestyle that Zaino lived; one that included spending money on a condominium in the Caribbean, high performance cars, and "a younger woman who was not his wife. Popeo was especially intrigued by $150,000 that Zaino had kept in banks in St. Marten and Florida. Zaino told the prosecutors that he had won the money gambling, but Popeo said that his private investigators could find no such evidence – not at casinos at Foxwoods, Atlantic City, or Las Vegas; not at racetracks throughout New England; not even with underworld bookies."[175]

As the trial approached in 1996, Popeo felt the outcome of the case was still very much in doubt. He was unable to find the "smoking gun" needed to destroy the state's case. "Then, on the eve of the trial, in May 1996, the prosecutors gave the DiPrete lawyers some documents that they said they had just found – including previously undisclosed statements from Brusini and Zaino. (The prosecutors would later point to their provision of this material to underscore their contention that they had not deliberately withheld evidence) The two defense lawyers immediately filed another motion for discovery. In response, the state handed over even more documents. But still missing was the document showing the state's agreement for immunity from perjury for Brusini. Astrachan insisted that the defense had everything. The debate came to a head during a July 25, 1996 conference call that resulted in Judge Cresto again ordering all prosecution documents turned over to him for review. Gina Merandi, the state police custodian of the records, informed DeCaporale that there were still some 30 boxes of material in her custody. Defense lawyers were overwhelmed at what they were presented with a few days later when they arrived at the Attorney General's office. "The boxes contained 68,000 pages of documents; just to copy them would cost $20,000.[176]

On August 16, 1996, Popeo and Egbert asked Judge Cresto to dismiss all charges on the grounds of prosecutorial misconduct. Once again, the prosecution denied withholding evidence and said that they had handed over all documents crucial to the case. The defense said the new material contained the first clues that Brusini had lied to a Grand Jury – when he denied any ownership interest in a building he had rented to the state, and that he had been given an undisclosed promise of immunity by the state. "Brusini's lie, and the state promise not to prosecute him, came to overshadow the question of the guilt or innocence of former Governor Edward D. DiPrete and his son Dennis L. DiPrete."[177]

On October 21, 1996, Judge Cresto began the hearing on the defense motion to dismiss the case. Kathleen Hagerty was assigned to represent the prosecution at the hearing. Hagerty had a reputation for working hard to prepare for her cases. She had won some major convictions including a case against a former Pawtucket special prosecutor, Frank Mattera, of soliciting a bribe to fix a drunk driving charge. But, she had earned some critics in the process. Four judges told Judge Joseph F. Rodgers, Jr., that "Hagerty was self-righteous and pushy – both with opposing lawyers and with witnesses."[178] On this day, she chose to argue that Judge Cresto had no right to even be hearing this motion. "The state, she said, denied any prosecutorial misconduct. But even if the prosecutors had 'secreted evidence,' she said, 'the remedies are quite limited. And in fact Your Honor may not impose sanctions' to penalize the prosecutors."[179]

◆————————————————◆

The State Attempts To Make Ratcliffe Take The Hit For Withholding Information

A few days before, Richard Ratcliffe had a lunch meeting with Hagerty and DeCaporale. During that meeting, both lawyers pressed Ratcliffe about the immunity deal he made with Brusini. They asked Ratcliffe if he had ever informed anyone else within the office about the deal. Ratcliffe insisted that he had, but in later testimony said that as a result of the questioning, he had gotten the clear impression that he was going to be used as a scapegoat and that everyone else would deny having any knowledge of the deal.

The defense called their first witness, Brusini lawyer, Richard A. Gonnella. He testified that his very first action was to insist on an immunity deal against his client for any perjury charges that might be pursued. He explained that he worked out such an arrangement with Ratcliffe and told DeCaporale about it. While Gonnella was still on the stand, state investigators called Ratcliffe and asked if he could come to the courthouse. He was the only person that could verify or refute what Gonnella was saying. Ratcliffe insisted he couldn't get to the courthouse. A few minutes later, the investigator walked into Ratcliffe's office and handed him a subpoena. Ratcliffe arrived in the courthouse and waited. He was eventually allowed to leave. The next day he showed up at the Attorney General's office to review documents for his testimony. While there, Pine and his Deputy, Thomas M. Dickinson, appeared and asked Ratcliffe about the immunity deal that had been arranged for Brusini. They were splitting hairs about whether Ratcliffe had made a promise or offered a reward or inducement. To Ratcliffe, there was no difference. However, Ratcliffe did tell Hagerty that James Ryan had notes from the meeting at which they discussed immunity that would show that Pine and Dickinson were in attendance. Even though he intended for Hagerty to use that information to turn the notes over to DiPrete's attorneys, the AG's office waited 10 more days before telling them about the notes.

Ratcliffe testified that before he left the Attorney General's office, he walked Astrachan through all the DiPrete files and recently called him to advise him to "amend the state's written declarations to reflect the Brusini perjury promise."[180] Astrachan denied that Ratcliffe ever told him that. Astrachan was on the witness stand for 6 days; being grilled first by Egbert and then by Popeo. "Suddenly, it seemed, it was the good guys who were on trial."[181] It was Astrachan's signature that appeared on most of the signed documents indicating that all documents had been turned over to the defense. He was now saying that he hadn't read all the material, he simply signed the papers "'as a matter of convenience. Astrachan was actually admitting that he and his fellow prosecutors had erred in swearing to the court that they had turned over all the evidence. And, he said, the prosecutors had been wrong to attack the DiPrete lawyers as incompetent liars for having said that evidence had been withheld.' "[182]

Astrachan was getting destroyed on the stand. DeCaporale would later say "that he never should have let 'the kid' sign the papers."[183] Hagerty was concerned about how the defense lawyers were making him look. During a sidebar, she expressed concern to Judge Cresto that the lawyers were setting Astrachan up for disciplinary action.

But there would be no rest for Astrachan. Popeo took the next shot, getting him to admit that the AG knew about the bank accounts that Frank Zaino, the key witness against Dennis DiPrete, opened in his children's names to hide money from his wife during the divorce. Even though the asset-reporting forms for divorce cases are signed under oath, the AG's office took no action against him and never notified the Family Court.

It was the testimony of Michael Burns, though, that really set the prosecution's case on its ear. Burns took with him to the stand "a detailed memo that summarized the DiPrete investigation. The memo had been written by the original prosecutor on the case, J. Richard Ratcliffe, and given to Jeffery Pine when Pine succeeded James O'Neil as Attorney General, in 1993. When Pine took office, Brusini was seeking immunity for various crimes, but no deal had been struck. 'We were prepared to indict Brusini for perjury and ethics violations,' Ratcliffe's memo said. Prosecutor Burns, under questioning by DiPrete lawyer Richard M. Egbert, conceded that he and Attorney General Pine had both read the memo in January 1993. But Burns said he'd forgotten about it until he rediscovered it, just the week before. When DeCaporale had learned about Burn's memo just moments before Burns took the stand, he said, "This is going to look bad."[184] Burns was on the stand for 11 days spread over several weeks but became ill before completing his testimony. He was replaced by James Ryan who testified "Pine and his prosecutors had discussed the possibility of offering Rodney Brusini immunity from perjury charges."[185]Burns eventually returned to the stand, but things didn't get any better for the prosecution. At one point Burns testified that he had just recently found out that there were several boxes of audiotapes of Brusini's Grand Jury. He eventually handed over 20 tapes to Judge Cresto. Ratcliffe, however, testified that he told Burns about the tapes and instructed him to turn them over to DiPrete's lawyers.

On another day, the court was told of 11 spiral bound notebooks of notes taken by Peter Blessing, one of the original investigators. Gina Merandi found them in a file cabinet drawer. Merandi testified that Astrachan lied when he said that the DiPretes lawyers now had all the evidence to which they were entitled. She also told about Burns, Astrachan and DeCaporale culling through evidence instead of providing everything to Cresto. For her efforts, she was called to state police headquarters where she was read her rights and told she was a suspect in the crimes of obstructing justice and perjury relating to her finding the 11 notebooks. She was never charged, but she was removed from the DiPrete case.

Cresto was not happy about what he was hearing. He "knew that the public expected the DiPretes to stand trial. Their indictment, in 1994, for bribery, racketeering, extortion, and perjury represented one of the biggest public-corruption cases in Rhode Island history. The thought of dismissing corruption charges against a former governor before a jury could hear the evidence did not sit well with the judge. Moreover, Cresto's earlier dismissal of part of the DiPrete case had been overturned by the state Supreme Court. Yet, in failing to turn over the evidence, the prosecutors had violated the judge's orders, the rules of the Rhode Island courts, and the U.S. Constitution. And that was something Dominic Cresto was not going to tolerate."[186]

◆————————————————————◆

Pine Removes Burns, DeCaporale and Astrachan From The Case, But Can't Stop The Judge From Ruling For The Defense

"On February 17, 1997, Pine announced he was replacing the prosecutors in the DiPrete case. Pine said he was making the change because 'it is clear' that the DiPrete lawyers may try to call prosecutors Michael Burns, Joseph DeCaporale, and Bruce Astrachan as witnesses in

It was widely speculated at the time whether Attorney General Violet would have supported the plea agreement that allowed Governor Di-Prete to serve only 1 year in prison while allowing Dennis to avoid jail time altogether. (1985 photo)

the trial, which would prevent them from serving as advocates for the state...The new prosecution team would be Assistant Attorneys General J. Patrick Youngs III, Michael J. Stone and Special Assistant Attorney General Kathleen M. Hagerty."[187]

March 11, 1997 turned out to be the last day of the 32-day pretrial hearing. Cresto asked his court secretary to type up the 38-page decision. While not ruling on the DiPretes' guilt or innocence, Cresto wrote, "The manner and magnitude of the prosecutorial misconduct found by the court to exist in this case has not only resulted in substantial prejudice to the defendants, but has the effect of eroding confidence in the criminal justice system."[188] He noted that the state had "repeatedly violated his orders, the state-court rules, the U.S. Constitution, and their own agreements with the DiPrete lawyers to give them critical pieces of evidence. 'The situation raises the alarming specter that the system works only if an accused has the financial resources to make independent investigation prior to trial to ferret out misconduct, to endure due process. 'Dismissal of the case,' Cresto wrote, was the only way 'to impress upon the prosecution that it cannot be allowed to benefit from having acted in a manner that is less than constitutional and ethical in the pursuit of convictions."[189]Just like that, the case against the DiPretes seemed to be over.

◆————————————————————◆

The Rhode Island Supreme Court Weighs In On The DiPrete Case As A Former Prosecutor Commits Suicide

Attorney General Pine saw it as his final chance to bring Governor DiPrete and his son Dennis to trial. "And so the accused and their accusers, the lawyers, the families, the investigators, and the curious gathered on Wednesday morning, November 12, 1997, for the oral arguments in the prosecutors' appeal of the dismissal of the corruption case against the DePretes."[190] As the Justices took their seats, the arguments began.

It had taken four years to reach this point and now all Michael Burns could do was stand, arms folded, in the rear of the courtroom. It was apparently more than he could bear. "Either late Saturday night or early Sunday morning of the week before Thanksgiving, the Chief of the Attorney General's Criminal Division walked into the snow covered woods near his secluded Johnston home and fired a single gunshot into his head. Thirty-nine year old Burns was dead from suicide.

The Supreme Court, based on the arguments just presented, would decide if the DiPretes would go on trial. "Chief Justice Joseph R. Weisberger, 77, was keenly aware of the public's cynicism toward government, having served through scandals that had toppled his two predecessors, Joseph A. Bevilacqua and Thomas F. Fay. When Weisberger succeeded Fay, in 1993, he had pledged to restore public confidence in the Rhode

Island Judiciary.[191]" He wanted desperately to do that when he suggested that he and his associates "reinstate the charges, so that the DiPretes could go to trial. He argued that Superior Court Judge Dominic F. Cresto had had no authority to dismiss the case."[192] Weisberger didn't want to punish the people of Rhode Island because of mistakes that may have been made by the state; mistakes that were eventually corrected, ultimately causing no harm to the defense team.

But Justice John P. Bourcier disagreed. Long considered "the brains on the trial court," Bourcier had a reputation for handing out stiff sentences. But he was a relatively new member of the Supreme Court. He argued that the case should be thrown out because of the misbehavior of the prosecutors. Cresto, he argued, had been within his authority and supported his position with state and federal case law. "If the Supreme Court ruled otherwise, Bourcier said, it would be bending the law to achieve a politically popular result: a trial of the DiPretes."[193]

The case would now be up to the three remaining Justices to decide. But two of the members had conflicts. Robert Flanders had served as DiPrete's legal counsel while Maureen McKenna Goldberg had been appointed to the Court by DiPrete. Each had to be recused from participation. To replace them, Weisberger chose retired Supreme Court Justices Florence K. Murray and Donald F. Shea to hear the case. Victoria S. Lederberg, a former state senator, was the other member.

Despite some "friction between Murray and Weisberger" in the past, Murray agreed with him on this issue. Lederberg, on the other hand, seemed to support

Bourcier's position. The case, in essence, now came down to the feelings of Donald Shea and he agreed with Weisberger and Murray."The DiPrete case had gained new life. On January 9, 1998, the Rhode Island Supreme Court issued a one-page order reinstating the charges against Edward and Dennis DiPrete."[194]

◆──────────────────◆

The ACLU Asks The Supreme Court
To Investigate The Attorney General

In February of 1994, Pine still had a 60% approval rating according to Brown University polling data. "But controversy over Pine's narcotics Strike Force and the DiPrete case have raised questions about Pine's judgment and generated the criticism that the Attorney General does not always fight fair."[195] Now, the ACLU asked the Supreme Court's Disciplinary Board to determine if Pine had acted inappropriately in the DiPrete case. Pine responded that the complaint was without merit because David Curtin of the Disciplinary Board had already informed the AG's staff that there were no improprieties in the DiPrete case. Curtin, however, insisted the matter was still under review and that there would be a lot more to come. Pine's Strike Force was also experiencing problems with informants and a case was dismissed as a result. FBI agents actually removed boxes of files from Pine's office and assumed authority over the case.

On March 4, 1998, Attorney General Pine said that he would not seek re-election to the position that he had held six years. He felt it was time to re-enter private practice where he could earn significantly more than the $55,000 he was making as Attorney General.

"Eight years after the first tip reached investigators, the case of the State vs. DiPrete"[196] still had not gone to trial and the new Superior Court Judge, Francis J. Darigan, Jr., had a new issue to deal with at a hearing before the lower court. This time the DiPrete attorneys were asking the court to award $1.2 million that it cost their clients to have them pour through 600 boxes of documents for items that were never handed over. They noted that the DiPretes had incurred legal fees exceeding $3 million to date. In addition to the money issue, Kathleen Hagerty continued to irritate the court when she explained to Darigan that her office disagreed with the Supreme Court. The prosecutors, she said, had not engaged in misconduct in the discovery process. "The Judge, peering over his reading glasses, ordered Hagerty to sit down. 'I don't need to be lectured by you, Miss Hagerty, on what constitutes discovery.' "[197]

◆————————————————————◆

The DiPretes Strike A Plea
Denying The People Of The State A Trial

Judge Darigan set a trial date of January 4, 1999, but on December 11, 1998, after almost four years of proclaiming their innocence, the DiPretes stunned the people of Rhode Island by deciding to accept a plea. Former Governor "Edward DiPrete pleaded guilty to 18 felony counts

of racketeering, extortion and bribery, as part of a plea-bar-
gain with state prosecutors. In the same courtroom, Dennis
DiPrete, who stood accused of being his father's bagman,
pleaded guilty to one misdemeanor charge of soliciting an
illegal $1,000 campaign contribution. He paid a $1,000
fine. As part of the deal, then-Attorney General Jeffrey B.
Pine agreed to drop all of the felony charges against Dennis. In accepting the pleas, Superior Court Judge Francis
J. Darigan, Jr. told Edward DiPrete: 'You have forever dis-
graced a proud family name and have caused you and your
family to suffer humiliation and derision solely because of
your surrender to greed and avarice. More importantly,'
Darigan said, 'you have broken faith with the Rhode Island
community, which on three occasions honored you by election to Rhode Island's highest public office. You have betrayed the public trust bestowed upon you, and this is most
reprehensible and contemptible.' "[198]

DiPrete was sentenced to 1 year in prison. He was
allowed to work at his family's insurance company during
the day, and was confined to prison at night and on week-
ends. He would serve only 11 months in prison before being
released early.

◆————————————————◆

Retirement Board Revokes
Ex-Governor's Pension
While Dennis Expands His Asset Base

But for Ed DiPrete, the struggle wasn't over. "The former Governor lost his license to sell insurance, and in January

1999, the state Retirement Board moved to strip him of his pension, which he had been receiving for eight years."[199] DiPrete had accumulated the pension serving in a long list of public service jobs that started with his service on the Cranston School Committee. His career brought him to the City Council and the Mayor's office and then to the Governor's office. He also served in the United States Navy. His annual state pension was $50,777. When his pension was finally revoked in November of 1999, DiPrete had already collected $380,613.75. "In revoking the pension, Presiding Justice Joseph F. Rodgers, Jr., cited DiPrete's dishonorable service as Governor, calling his crimes "both extraordinary and unprecedented."[200] Rodgers agreed with Patricia DiPrete's claim that she was an innocent spouse, however, he said she wasn't entitled to any part of the pension because neither she nor her husband had provided enough information on her financial condition. Even as the former Governor was led into the courtroom in shackles, he refused, on at least a dozen occasions, to discuss his family finances, invoking his Fifth Amendment rights on advise of legal counsel. Since his release from prison, DiPrete has limited any discussion of his finances to his legal defense debts, which totaled over $1 million. By 2004, Edward and Patricia DiPrete had sold about $2 million worth of real estate they owned. The DiPretes appealed the pension ruling to the RI Supreme Court.

But while the former Governor was liquidating assets, Dennis and his wife were scooping them up. In debt to the tune of over $3 million in legal defense bills, Dennis DiPrete and/or his wife, Susan, have acquired two water view lots off Ocean Road in Narragansett. They built a fairly extensive home on one of the lots, a house that has 12 rooms, 5 bedrooms and 4 ½ baths and, according to sources, a home movie theater in the basement. A staff member in the office of the Narragansett Tax Assessor "calls it 'the nicest estate in Narragansett.' "[201] The 2000 tax assessment totaled $2,855,700 with an annual tax bill of $18,051.78 that was paid in full in advance. The Di-Pretes paid $650,000 for the raw land. The title to the property is held in the SFD Trust created by Susan DiPrete. WBR LLC purchased the second lot. Dennis paid $600,000 for that piece in February of 2001. Even before Dennis took ownership, he received an offer to purchase from Dennis Grey, a Lincoln contractor, who offered $875,000. DiPrete later rejected the offer and was sued by the contractor. Dennis' brother, Thomas, an attorney, valued the property at $1.2 million in court documents. The parties reached an out of court settlement.

Stories of traditional political corruption, both active and passive as exemplified in these stories, make headlines somewhere in the world almost on a daily basis. They are intriguing to read and almost hypnotic in their ability to breed complacency on the part of the electorate. The effects of traditional political corruption are many and devastating. From lost economic opportunity to higher taxes to a distrust of government and politicians, traditional political corruption tears at the fabric of our society leaving only disappointment and economic destruction in its wake.

PART II

CIRCUMSTANTIAL POLITICAL CORRUPTION

As discussed earlier, political corruption comes in various forms. While not all forms of corruption are illegal and/or prosecutable, almost all forms share common characteristics which may render them immoral and/or unethical. Municipally elected and appointed public officials take an oath of office that requires adherence to the Constitution of the United States, the Constitution of the State of Rhode Island, and the governing local municipal charter. Citizens deserve and expect that all duties of their elected and appointed officials will be discharged honestly and in accordance with the requirements of the law. Government, as everyone knows, does not always work that way. Many public officials, probably the vast majority of them, are honest, but their work is often overshadowed by the acts of officials that are greedy and self-serving. And like corruption itself, greed and selfishness have a negative impact on society as a whole. The following stories are not isolated and occur repeatedly over time in various local government scenarios. Both describe some form of Circumstantial Political Corruption; that is, a local official using the power of his/her position, in violation of the oath of office and the guidelines of the position, so as to benefit either personally, financially or politically.

4

"IT'S NOT MY LOAN"

North Providence Acting Finance Director Maria Vallee

As 2006 drew to a close, former North Providence Town Councilman Robert DiStefano decided to retire from his position as the Town's Finance Director. He held the job for a number of years but, with the impending change of administration brought about by the November election of current Mayor A. Ralph Mollis as Rhode Island's 27th Secretary of State, this apparently seemed like the right time to retire from town service. Rather than fill the position, newly elected Mayor Charles A. Lombardi left the post vacant, choosing instead to elevate DiStefano's understudy, Maria Vallee, to the position in an acting capacity.

A relatively petite woman, Vallee had little problem exercising the authority afforded the finance director. According to one long-time town hall employee, the once sweet and disarming Vallee became a venomous object of trepidation creating apprehension and anxiety among fellow employees. It was no surprise then, that Vallee's coworkers would vocally complain about Vallee's perceived indiscretions.

The North Providence Town Hall where Maria Vallee was accused of improperly taking a HUD loan meant for low income residents of the town.

During an impromptu meeting with Councilman Mansuet Guisti in June 2010, Councilman Frank Manfredi learned that several "women in the Town Hall" were complaining about a loan that Vallee received from the federal department of Housing and Urban Development (HUD) through a program administered by the Town. The program, intended to provide home repair loans for low-income families, was not meant for someone with a salary in the high $70 thousand range, and the others felt that she had inappropriately taken advantage of her position to obtain loan funds for which she was not qualified at the exclusion of other individuals that may have been in greater need. To make matters worse, some believed that other town hall employees were covering up her indiscretions by failing to record the loan in the land evidence records, as required under the program guidelines, and not enforcing the repayment policy resulting in a loan payment delinquency of several months.

Manfredi believed that the activity was potentially criminal and needed to be investigated. Just a month earlier, in May of 2010, three councilmen, including the council president, were indicted on bribery and conspiracy charges and resigned their council positions. If town hall were really a hotbed of political corruption, as many now believed, Manfredi was determined that the cleansing would start here and now. He brought his grievance to the full Town Council and asked that the Finance Committee, normally a four-member panel that he chaired, be authorized to conduct an investigation. The depleted four member council gave its unanimous approval to proceed. Despite the unanimous council support, cooperation from the Lombardi Administration was not forthcoming. A letter request for the production of documents was ignored as was a subsequent formal request under the state's Access to Public Records Act (APRA). Formal subpoenas issued by the council finally netted thousands of pages of documents, many irrelevant and perhaps intended to consume hours of investigative time by the members of the part-time Finance Committee.

For three months Manfredi and his colleagues scoured through the documents trying to piece together the HUD loan puzzle. The information was very telling and helped make it clear to some of the council members why certain members of the Town Administration were reluctant to provide the documents. There was now every reason to believe that some of the activity related to Vallee's HUD loan violated HUD's Program Rules and Regulations, RI Ethics Laws and potentially constituted criminal activity on the part of Vallee and other high ranking members of the Lombardi Administration. One would think that such evidence would be embraced and acted upon by the other council members and the Mayor, but that was not the case. As the Finance Committee members weeded through the boxes of documents a sense of clarity began to develop and the activities of the acting Finance Director started to fall into place. The Administration continued to stonewall and Councilman Giusti, who was now serving as the Council President, began to oppose the Committee's efforts to obtain the facts.

The Finance Committee issued a subpoena to Maria Vallee to appear at a hearing to answer questions about her role in the HUD loan program, but she refused to appear thereby denying the Committee of her perspective. Manfredi, along with this book's co-author, former Councilman Paul F. Caranci, spent over a hundred man hours researching, writing, and assembling documentation for a 140 page report describing in detail the irregularities in the Vallee HUD loan.

The report was presented to, and accepted by, the Finance Committee in September 2010. Giusti, who was once an ally in the effort to uncover any wrongdoing in the granting of the loan, was now opposing the committee's activities with increased regularity, at times working to discredit its content and conceal its findings. Despite his lack of cooperation, the report was accepted by the full Council and revealed the following:

- A HUD loan was granted to a town employee by the town's HUD Loan Committee. The Loan Committee was comprised of three town employees that included Rocco Gesualdi, Director of Administration, Maria Vallee, Acting Finance Director and Sherri Arlia. HUD regulations disqualify employees from eligibility in the program. They further disqualify any member of the Loan Committee from eligibility.

- HUD Regulations reserve all funds for persons with aggregate annual household income of $58,550 or less. Maria Vallee earned in excess of $70,000 in her role as acting finance director. The Vallee's reported combined family income was $125,000. The Vallee's total household income exceeded the annual limit by a factor of more than two.

- Vallee sought to circumvent the income limit guidelines by failing to include her name on the application pretending instead to present her husband as the sole applicant. Evidence existed however that the Committee had previously rejected applicants because their household income exceeded the guidelines suggesting that Vallee and the other

Committee members were very familiar with the family income limitation requirement.

- The loan granted to the Vallees exceeded HUD's guidelines. HUD regulations limit the size of home improvement fund loans to $12,500 per unit. Under special circumstances (which did not exist in this case) the committee may grant loans exceeding $12,500 per unit. No other loans granted by the North Providence Loan Committee exceeded the $12,500 cap. The Vallee loan exceeded the cap by a factor of more than three.

- Checks written to pay contractors for work done on the Vallee home were signed by Maria Vallee despite the fact that she claimed to have recused herself from the process to feign avoidance of impropriety. In some cases the funds were provided to the vendors even before the loan was officially approved.

- Maria Vallee directed the department that was in charge of collecting payments from loan recipients. The Vallee loan was at one-time 9 months delinquent in payments yet no action was taken by that department to collect the arrearage. Within two months of the start of the Finance Committee's investigation, all past due payments were made by Maria Vallee in an apparent effort to conceal the delinquency and all the checks were signed by her, not her husband, despite her insistence that the loan was not hers. This latter justification was repeated many times throughout the course of the investigation by Lombardi's Chief of Staff G. Richard Fossa.

- Inspections of the work completed at the Vallee home were not performed by town officials in a timely manner despite the vendors having already been paid in full for their work. This is a clear violation of HUD guidelines, which requires that satisfactory inspections be performed prior to the contractor getting paid. In an apparent attempt to conceal this breach of HUD requirements, there was an attempt to backdate some of the inspection reports.

- The lien on the Vallee property was not recorded until some 18 months after the loan was approved leaving HUD totally exposed for the repayment of their funds for that length of time and constituting a violation of the program guidelines.[202]

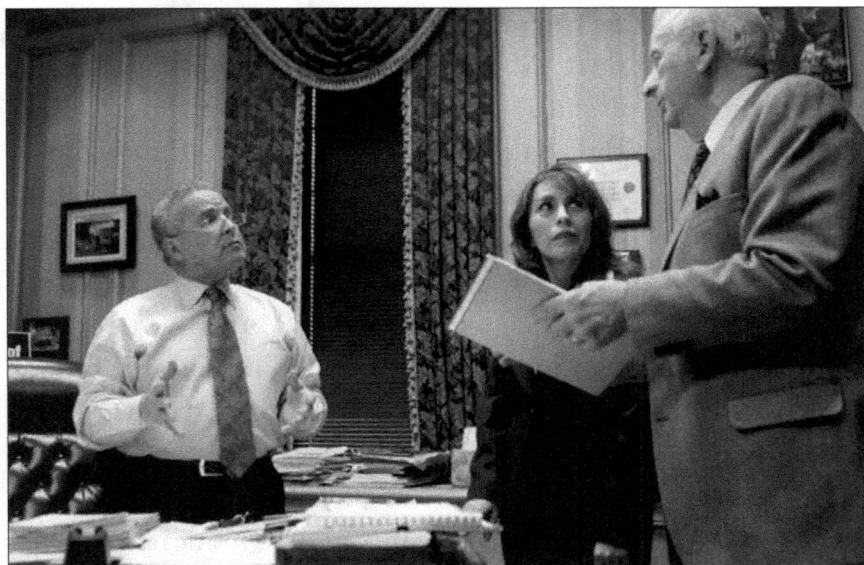

*Mayor Charles Lombardi, Maria Vallee and Richard Fossa
meet in the mayor's office..*

The report recommended that the council invoke its powers under the Town Charter to place Maria Vallee and Sherri Arlia, a member of the HUD Loan Committee, on administrative leave until the HUD Office of Inspector

General (OIG) had an opportunity to complete its investigation of the program. The report concluded that no action needed to be taken against Rocco Gesualdi, the Mayor's former Director of Administration, since he had already left the employ of the town. The Committee voted to refer the report, with its recommendations, to the full council for action. The council, which now included three new members elected to replace the three members who resigned, accepted the report, but on a vote of 5-2, refused to take the recommended action opting instead to first let the federal investigation conclude,[203] despite Manfredi's and Caranci's insistance that the two actions were not related and one should not prevent the other.

For their part, Maria Vallee and her husband Michael, who was officially listed on the HUD application as the recipient of the loan, lawyered up immediately upon being accused. Maria retained Anthony M. Traini while James Lepore represented Michael. Each lawyer had ties to Local 1033 of the RI Laborers Union that represents Town Hall employees. For her part, Maria Vallee contended that the loan was compliant with all federal guidelines since it was in her husband's name and his income alone did not exceed HUD's guidelines.

Mayor Lombardi went out of his way, according to sources within Town Hall, to conceal any evidence of Vallee's involvement in the transaction. He held at least two meetings with staffers who, according to some of those in attendance, were essentially sessions on how to best protect Vallee from prosecution. In addition he attended a meeting of several Administration members with Frank Manfredi and Manny Giusti ostensibly to answer questions about the loan program. However, Vallee was excluded from the meeting and those in attendance provided few answers. Town Solicitor Anthony Gallone, who had requested the services of a court stenographer to record and transcribe the proceedings, tempered any answers that were forthcoming according to some of those present.[204]

After completing an investigation based in part on a review of all the information that Manfredi and Caranci provided to the council, Michael Tondra of the state Office of Housing and Community Development, the state agency that administers the federal money on

The front and rear view of the house owned by Vallee who was accused of improperly taking a HUD loan for which she was not eligible. Vallee, in a plea deal with federal investigators, agreed to pay a substantial penalty for her actions.

HUD's behalf, closed down the federal loan program in North Providence. He ordered Vallee and other employees who received a HUD loan in violation of program guidelines to immediately return all of the money they received. In his report, Tondra observed, "several government employees have received housing rehabilitation loans in the past, in at least one instance, a local employee (a reference to Maria Vallee) who directly exercises responsibilities with regard to the Community Development Block Grant Program (CDBG), received loan assistance. In this instance, the town has indicated the individual recused themselves from any discussion related to the loan. No formal documentation of the recusal was available. At no time has the town requested exception from conflict of interest provisions for any individual...Provision of assistance to government employees, particularly those who exercise functions or responsibilities with respect to CDBG activities, and/or those with whom they have family/business ties, without written exception, violates CDBG conflict of interest provisions. Recusal alone, even if documented appropriately, is insufficient to comply with this requirement." The agency's report was delivered to the town in early August and Mayor Lombardi announced that the town was "preparing a corrective action plan in response to the Office of Housing and Community Development's recent investigation of the HUD program."[205]

In addition to the findings already noted, the Office of Housing and Community Development's report reviewed many inconsistencies within the town records on the eligibility of loan recipients. It identified several instances of conflict of interest and gave the town 30 days to submit documents verifying the eligibility of 29 loan recipients. It also found that Maria Vallee had written checks to her-self.[206]

Lombardi took the opportunity to announce that he might place the program under the direction of Tri-Town, a community action program that helps low income residents of North Providence and Johnston but claimed the program was still running, a claim that contradicted the HUD OIG report and the facts. Despite the many legal problems and the discontinuation of the program that left many low income residents without the type of emergency help afforded by the Community Development Block Grant Program, the Mayor continued to protect Vallee and defend her actions still refusing to consider taking any disciplinary action against her.

Council President Giusti, for his part, opposed any disciplinary hearings at the council level saying that he preferred that the outside agencies, the RI Ethics Commission and HUD, conduct their own investigations. As if to borrow from the talking points of Mayor Lombardi, he noted, *"I just think we should be done with it. Once it's in the hands of the authorities, we should be done with it."* Giusti also contended that Manfredi and Caranci would expose the town to legal action if the character of two employees were discussed at public meetings.[207] In fact, Manfredi and Caranci were seeking executive sessions for that purpose and that is the lawful forum in which to discuss personnel matters. The council, however, sided with Giusti thereby preventing the council from discussing the matter. Those council members apparently failed to understand Manfredi's and Caranci's contention that the North Providence Town Charter grants the council its own legal authority and responsibility to take action when misconduct by town personnel is identified.

Neither Manfredi nor Caranci ran for reelection in 2010 and each left the council in January 2011 when their terms expired. Their departure signaled the end of the Council's investigation into local corruption in North Providence. Fortunately, the work of federal and state authorities continued. On July 9, 2013, a complaint was filed in federal district court by the US Attorney seeking damages, civil penalties, and recovery of wrongfully paid monies, from Maria Vallee under the False Claims Act based upon false claims and statements made by "Vallee acting in deliberate ignorance of the truth or falsity of the information in order to obtain payment of HUD Community Block Grant (CDBG) funds..." The complaint noted Maria Vallee intentionally violated the terms of the HUD program guidelines to enrich herself since at all material times, Vallee "had access to and was presumed to be familiar with the rules and regulations governing the CDBG program, and any failure on her part to know the application of the program guidelines to her loan application was in deliberate ignorance of the truth or falsity of the information that was available to her." The complaint also cited Vallee's inappropriate use of the funds for cosmetic improvements to her home that also breached the program guidelines.[208]

Though the government's charges might have amounted to a criminal indictment, the US Attorney, after substantial discussions and negotiations with the Vallees' attorneys, settled for a single count civil complaint that required the payment of "triple the amount of single damages of $47,895 plus civil penalties of $5,500 to $11,000 for each false claim submitted, as permitted by law, the cost of the action, plus interest..."

In the end, the federal action was settled with the entry of a consent judgment that required Vallee to admit to violating the False Claims Act by presenting false claims for payment or approval to an agent of the United States, and ordered her to pay $78,292.50 for her part in the HUD loan scandal in addition to having reimbursed the town $47,895, the amount of the original loan.[209]

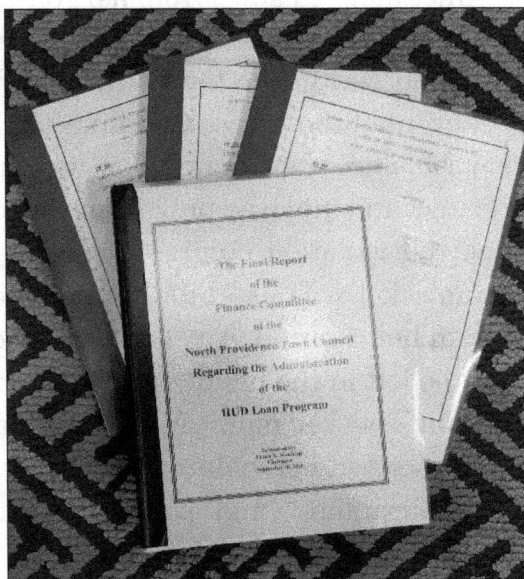

The report of the Finance Committee's investigation into the Vallee HUD loan that was submitted to the town council. The town council refused to act on the report's recommendation.

With the federal charges resolved, the Rhode Island Ethics Commission was free to address Vallee's serious breach of Rhode Island's Ethics laws. Acknowledging the "totality of circumstances," RI Ethics Commission staff attorney Jason Gramitt reported that 47 year old Vallee agreed to pay an $8,000 fine for recklessly disregarding state ethics standards by improperly receiving an illegal federal loan geared for families of low and moderate income. Vallee also acknowledged her violation of relevant state laws.[210]

Vallee's admission of wrongdoing and her violation of federal and state law left many North Providence residents expecting her resignation or dismissal from her town hall job. In June 2011, just hours before the RI Ethics Commission had found probable cause for numerous alleged ethical and statutory violations Vallee stepped down from her role as Acting Finance Director and returned to her job as town controller, still a substantial position within the town's finance department. Vallee's action prevented the Ethics Commission from removing her from her job since the Commission has the authority under law to remove an employee only from the job that was held at the time the violation occurred. Because of the job change the Commission was essentially prevented from removing Vallee from her position. Any decision for disciplinary action would now be left in the hands of Mayor Lombardi.

In a move that shocked many, Mayor Lombardi refused to fire Vallee. He described her violations as "lapses in an otherwise 'stellar' performance" and pointed out that "these lapses did not result in any criminal prosecution. 'I think she suffered enough,' Lombardi said."

A private citizen's attempt to have Vallee removed from office citing a provision of the Town Charter failed when the Town's Personnel Board ruled that the petition was not timely filed. The Town Council again steadfastly refused to take a position on the citizen's actions.

The refusal of the Mayor coupled with the refusal of the new Town Council to act in accordance with their powers under the Town Charter, essentially allowed an arguably corrupt individual to remain in a position of high authority within the town government administration. That is the precise impact that Councilmen Manfredi and Caranci anticipated and feared when they argued for strong and immediate council action in response to the Vallee corruption.

It would be unfortunate enough if the story ended here, but it does not. On November 19, 2015, Justin Cambio, the Town's new Finance Director hired by Lombardi in the fall of 2013 to fill the void left by Vallee, was arrested on felony charges after allegedly post betting at Twin River Casino in Lincoln, RI. Post betting is a form of cheating whereby the gambler adds to his earnings by placing more chips on a winning bet prior to being paid. Despite surveillance tape evidence at Twin River showing that Cambio's cheating was, according to State Police Maj. Joe Philbin, "very obvious," Lombardi again refused to immediately fire the Finance Director. Instead, the Mayor placed Cambio on administrative leave allowing Cambio to collect on his vacation and personal time. Incredibly, Maria Vallee was once again elevated to the position of Acting Finance Director. Essentially, Lombardi replaced a person who was alleged to have been cheating in a casino on his own personal time using his own personal money with a person who accepted responsibility for inappropriately taking government money while on the job and using her position to do it. Lombardi's Chief of Staff told NBC 10 in response to their inquiry that the administration stands by the decision. According to the news station, Fossa said, "(Vallee) may have been ill advised or made a mistake, but she was never delinquent on that loan, as soon as they inquired about it, she settled," said Fossa. When asked by the reporter "if the people of North Providence could trust Vallee with their money, Fossa replied, 'I would back her 100 percent.' "[41] Even at this juncture, the administration modifies the extent of Vallee's wrongdoing by attempting to rewrite very recent history. The facts show that Vallee was in fact very delinquent with her loan payments as noted earlier in this chapter.

Only time will tell what Lombardi will ultimately decide on the Cambio matter. In the meantime, North Providence residents are again left to ponder the question of how committed their government leaders are to the sound ethical standards required for the sound government administration of their tax dollars. The apparent selective enforcement of good government rules; the 50% tolerance, rather than no tolerance, of illegal behavior within the highest ranks of town government, sends a clear message to those who would consider taking part in illegal activity both on and off the job in North Providence. That message: Corruption of any kind will not be tolerated unless you are a friend or supporter of people in power. Clearly that is not the right message to send.

The active circumstantial political corruption on the part of Maria Vallee, indeed her failure to live up to the fiduciary responsibilities of her position, had a potentially significant negative impact to untold North Providence residents. It belittled a process and diminished citizen confidence in the political system. Just as egregious is the passive circumstantial corruption of many other town officials. Their refusal to acknowledge the infractions of law and the breaches of ethics as well as their refusal to do all that was possible to terminate Vallee's employment, fan the fires of those who would paint all politicians with the broad brush of corruption. Taken together, the active and passive actions of government leaders toward corruption tend to diminish property values, drive up taxes and reduce the overall quality of life in a small town.

5

THE BLOODLESS REVOLUTION

Governor Theodore Francis Green

One of the most intriguing developments in Rhode Island's political history, certainly the one that may have had the greatest immediate impact on the government as we know it today, may well be the Green coup of 1935 or "The Bloodless Revolution" as it has come to be known. On the first day of that year, the Democrats, in a political maneuver seemingly designed by Machiavelli himself, turned Rhode Island state government inside out.

To understand the passions that led to the events of January 1, 1935, it is important to first understand the political history of the time. Rhode Island had been under the firm grip of Republican machine politics since 1856. The Republican state legislature was the center of power that controlled, in grand machine style, everything that was important. During the Republican reign, the state was gerrymandered in such a way that in 1900, according to Erwin L. Lavine, 28 municipalities representing just 18% of the population elected 28 senators, nine more than a majority of the Senate. The ten largest municipalities, responsible for 82% of the population, elected only 10. "Even until 1957, only 3.7% of the state's population was able to elect over 30% of the Senate."[212] Because the political nature of the rural areas tends to be Republican, the Senate Republicans were able to easily defeat any legislation that they considered dangerous to their interests.[213]

General Charles Ray Brayton

In the early 1900's the Governor had little power. He had very little administrative authority under the constitution and could not veto legislation. He could make recommendations only and couldn't investigate any department or administration or demand reports without Senate approval. The Senate had to approve all measures passed by the House and had the power of appointment. The Senate, therefore, held the real power and it was under the control of machine boss General Charles Brayton "who traced his Rhode Island roots back to 1643 and the founding of his native Warwick."[214] He was heir to a very prominent family with a political history. His father, William, served the state as a two-term Republican Congressman from 1857 to 1861. Charles Brayton himself boasted a distinguished military career in the Civil War as both a General and the Chief political lieutenant of U.S. Senator Henry Bowen Anthony, the principal organizer of Rhode Island's Republican Party.

Anthony helped Brayton secure his own political positions that included U.S. Pension Agent for Rhode Island, U.S. Postmaster for Providence, and a long tenure as the Rhode Island Republican Party Chairman, a position he was able to maintain even though scandal chased him from his Postmaster position. His political career spanned four decades over which time he "manipulated the politics of Rhode Island as the prototypical boss of a highly successful rural-based political machine."[215]

Lavine tells how Brayton specialized in "buying the voters of the small towns." From his perch in the state house office of the High Sheriff of Providence, he barked his orders in military fashion. He was so much a part of the legislative session that *The Providence Journal* once ran a cartoon depicting Brayton leaving a padlocked state house after planting a sign on the lawn that gave his home address in case of emergency. The caption read "General Assembly Adjourns."

Providence Journal *cartoon of Charles Brayton showing the control he had over members of the RI General Assembly.*

One of the elements of his power was a 1901 law that bears his name. The Brayton Law of 1901 "made it impossible for a governor, whose legal powers of appointment were quite limited to begin with, to make any appointment without Brayton's consent."[216] The law required the Senate to act on any gubernatorial appointment within three days. If the Senate failed to act within the prescribed time, the governor lost his power to appoint and the Senate could then appoint its own nominee to the post. This assured that all patronage power for the entire state was in the control of the senate, not the governor. Rhode Island historian, Patrick T. Conley, notes that in addition to his leadership qualities and reputation as a "stern disciplinarian," Brayton's success was in "his ability to control the General Assembly through old-stock rural legislation from the country towns, because each of the state's municipalities, regardless of size, had one vote in the Senate."[217]

The State House, Providence, RI. -- site of the 1935 bloodless revolution.

In addition to the above, the Republican's power was also secured because 60% of the state's population "was disenfranchised until 1888. Until that time, only "native" males could vote which meant of course that the large immigrant populations of the cities were politically neutralized."[218] Even after the word "native" was stricken from the law in 1888, the already substantial property ownership requirement was not only maintained, but also strengthened to include elections of municipal council seats. Therefore, the immigrant population, while being allowed to vote in mayoral elections, still had no voice in the election of municipal councilors. This is significant because, unlike today, at that time, city councilmen, not the mayor, controlled city patronage. In addition to controlling state patronage then, the Republicans kept a firm grip on municipal patronage. No one could work at any level of government without the consent of the Republican Party bosses. This reach also extended deep into the private sector job market.

Finally, the Republicans controlled the finances upon which elections were run. Richard A. Gabriel, PhD, author of a University of Rhode Island Research Paper entitled The Political Machine in Rhode Island, explains that the "financial support was drawn from two outlets; first, sheriff's fees and kickbacks from patronage appointees and second, from the Hartford-New Haven railroads, banks, insurance companies, electric railway companies and mill owners. In short, the Republican machine extracted heavy fees from businessmen who wanted special favors. It was of course no accident that Brayton himself was the chief lobbyist for all these substantial business interests."[219]

With control over all patronage jobs, and with the financial ability to ensure the election or re-election of all its candidates, the Republican Party could virtually do whatever it pleased with no regard for the people and no fear of losing their positions.

Senators Theodore Francis Green, the architect of the Bloodless Revolution, poses with J. Howard McGrath, and President Harry S. Truman, October 28, 1948.

Slowly over time, however, the Democrats were able to make some inroads into the Republican control. Because the Republicans were entrenched in the suburban areas, the Democrats were forced to look for strength in the cities where ethnic immigrants were moving in large numbers. Yet, this new found Democratic base was ineligible to vote because of the disenfranchisement restrictions.

The Democratic cause was given a significant boost in 1928, however, when the property qualification for participation in the elections of councilmen was eliminated. At the same time, the nation was in the midst of the great depression. Nationally, "Franklin D. Roosevelt, through the creation of federal welfare programs, provided a source of relief and help to the traditional clients of the machine and thereby deprived the machine of much of its loyalty gained through the provision of social and economic services."[220] Add to these developments two close Senate races in the election of 1934, and the stage for the "revolution" was set.

In the years since 1928, operating on the strength of the new immigrant voters, the Democrat Party was becoming more organized and gaining General Assembly seats in each successive election. These were the conditions that Theodore Francis Green, a Democrat first elected governor in 1932, faced when he began his long career in Rhode Island politics. Functioning under the Brayton Law of 1901, he was powerless in the face of the Senate still under Republican rule.

In his re-election of 1934, Green found fortune in a Democrat takeover of the House of Representatives for the first time since the Civil War. The slim eight vote margin in the House assured that the cohesive, power-starved Democrats would emerge victorious on every vote. The Senate, however, was still under Republican domination, but by the slimmest of margins - two seats - with 22 seats being held by Republicans and 20 seats in Democrat hands.

Democrats, who for the first time in seventy-eight years were sensing that power was within their reach, would find a way to take advantage of election fraud allegations in the two close elections. In the Portsmouth Senate race, the Democrat lost by only 39 votes while in South Kingstown the Democrat lost by 61 votes. Allegations of fraud abounded in each of those races. Democrat Lt. Governor, Robert E. Quinn, described by United States Senator John O. Pastore as "a very forceful man and an idol of mine,"[221] refused to swear in the Republican winners until an investigation into the fraud charges could be conducted.

"There ensued a series of secret meetings at Green's home. Among the participants were Quinn, key Democrat legislators and US Attorney J. Howard McGrath. Seizing upon a constitutional provision making each legislative chamber the judge of the elections of its own members, Quinn came up with the strategy of having a special Senate committee recount the ballots in the Portsmouth and South Kingstown races. Everything was choreographed – as the Republicans were shocked to discover."[222]

Using the authority of his office, Lt. Gov. Quinn announced on the first day of the General Assembly session that in response to protests he received against the seating of Republican Senators elected from Portsmouth and South Kingstown, he would not swear them in until the allegations of fraud could be investigated and a recount of the ballots could be achieved. The Senate, therefore, was deadlocked at 20 Democrats and 20 Republicans. Lt. Gov. Quinn, a Democrat, would now be in a position of casting the tie-breaking vote on all matters. With little debate or fanfare, the Democrats took advantage of the stunned Republican Senators by establishing a three-member committee comprised of two Democrats and one Republican to count the ballots in the two disputed races. The Committee took to its charge immediately, and by evening of that same day, reported that the two Democrat challengers, and not the Republicans, had actually won the Senate elections in Portsmouth and South Kingstown.

The newly announced Democrat victors were sworn-in almost immediately and the coup was in full motion. One of the first acts of the new Democrat controlled Senate was to vacate all judicial appointments to the State Supreme

Court. Historian William G. McLoughlin told *Journal-Bulletin* Political Reporter M. Charles Bakst, "Once the Democrats put themselves in control of the court, the GOP would have no way to appeal the 'revolution' ".[223] Senator John O. Pastore, who told Bakst, that he didn't know about the revolution until the morning of the opening session, admitted that the "problem with the court was an old story."

T.F. Green 1935, fought corruption with corruption in the Bloodless Revolution.

Democrats thought the Supreme Court was very conservative, was anti-Democratic. Election cases that reached the court always went against the Democrats, and the resentment was 'brewing for a long period.' "[224] The measure to vacate the court was ushered through the Senate in just a few minutes.

The House of Representatives, while engaging in a livelier debate over the issue, came to the same conclusion. In that chamber, Republican Representative Walter Curry argued, "What are we coming to when not even the courts of the State are safe from patronage? There isn't one man in Rhode Island who can say one word against the integrity and ability of the present court and the honesty of each member. You even stoop to throwing the sop of a pension to justices if they withdraw immediately and no longer exercise their duties. You do that because you fear your own action tonight might be brought against that Supreme Court."[225]

Pawtucket Representative Harry F. Curvin, who would later become the longest serving House Speaker in Rhode Island history and then Chairman of the powerful RI Board of Elections, carried the Democrats water. He said in reply simply, "We are giving the people of the State what they requested by their votes on November 6th. The people last November voted for something more than mere candidates. They voted for what they had a right to have and they gave a mandate to the Democratic Party to give it to them."[226]

Just like that, Chief Justice Charles F. Stearns along with Associate Justices Elmer J. Rathbun, John W. Sweeney, John S. Murdock and J. Jerome Hahn, all Republicans, were voted off the Supreme Court.

Immediately following House support for the motion to declare the court vacant, and very late into the night, a Joint Session convened for the purpose of electing new members of the Rhode Island Supreme Court. House Majority Leader Edmund W. Flynn, at the urging of Pawtucket boss Thomas P. McCoy, and after threatening to interrupt Governor Green's reforms in the House if he weren't selected, was chosen as the new Chief Justice. Along with Flynn, Democrats Francis B. Condon and William W. Moss, and Republicans Hugh B. Baker and Antonio A. Capotosto were also appointed to the Court.

The Brayton Law, the law that essentially stripped the governor of his ability to make appointments providing that power to the Senate, was also promptly repealed.

Those who went to bed early on that 1st day of January 1935 would wake up the next morning to find out everything had changed. The Governor, the House of Representatives, the Senate and the State Supreme Court were now all under the firm control of the Democrat Party. Some 80 independent boards or commissions had been replaced with 11 departments of government also under control of the Democrats. While machine politics would still be the order of the day, the agenda of the new machine was dramatically different and the base of political power shifted from the rural areas to the urban centers.

Republicans held power for too long and power corrupts. The good people who held Republican control over the governmental system lost sight of why they held political office and of whom they were elected to serve. However, in seizing the opportunity to bring an end to what they perceived as a corrupt government, the Democrats resorted to political trickery, itself a form of corruption. They took advantage of the circumstances before them to wrest control of an entire government away from the Republicans whom the Democrats perceived as the real corrupt power brokers.

Two wrongs, as they say, don't make a right and the ends simply don't justify the means. The events of the Bloodless Revolution epitomize the meaning of circumstantial corruption.

PART III

SITUATIONAL POLITICAL CORRUPTION

The third form of political corruption is situational corruption. Like its close relative, circumstantial political corruption, the acts that define situational corruption may not be illegal. However, those corrupt acts are just as corrosive to society and the political process as the acts of circumstantial corruption. The violation of the public trust through the unjust acts of situational corruption often results in financial and personal hardship to the victim. There is a resulting loss of confidence by the victim, perhaps the entire society, in the political system and government becomes the object of distrust and ridicule. Even the honest service of hard working government officials is diminished as all politicians tend to be painted with the same broad brush strokes of their corrupt brethren. The two examples of situational corruption described on the following pages are endemic of a society motivated by greedy insiders who are more concerned about their own political sustenance than the well-being of the community they serve. The actions may be despicable and cause pain and suffering to the victims who are often times asking for no more than they rightfully are owed under the laws that govern the situation they find themselves in.

6

McMANSIONS

The Johnston Zoning Board

arol LaCourse had once owned her own home in Lincoln, but facing the reality of her second husband, Paul, being disabled from asbestosis from his years of work in the shipping industry, and the ever rising costs of health care and home ownership, the insulin dependent sixty seven year old decided that it was time to sell. The youngest of her six children, daughter Michelle, purchased the house in 2002 netting Carol a small profit. She and Paul temporarily moved in with her daughter Margie and son-in-law Paul Caranci (the co-author of this book.) The plan was to remain in Paul and Margie's North Providence home until her application for senior housing was approved allowing Carol and Paul LaCourse the opportunity to live in a North Providence government subsidized apartment. However, just over a year later, Paul LaCourse died derailing Carol's desire for senior housing.

On July 30, 2004, using most of the money she had received from the sale of her home, Carol purchased a small house and an adjoining lot in the Town of Johnston, just a few miles west of her daughter Margie. The seller, Thomas Blacke (also a co-author of this book), inherited his boyhood home following the death of his parents. Tom was married and living in Cranston so he decided to sell the house and the adjoining lot. He was told repeatedly by officials of the Town of Johnston that the vacant lot, despite being a separate lot of record that was taxed as a "buildable lot" was in fact not buildable without benefit of a zoning variance. After his Realtor confirmed the need for a variance, Blacke was forced to sell the two properties as a single package.

The Johnston Town Hall.

The Town of Johnston lies just west of North Providence and was incorporated in 1759 taking its name from a local politician, Attorney General Augustus Johnston, perhaps demonstrating just how seriously the Town regards its politics. Today, its approximately 28,000 residents enjoy relative financial stability emanating in part from a growing tax base. The improving financial outlook of the town, plus the fact that the house was situated right between a string of small, older homes lying to the north and some very large, much newer homes to the south and west made the property the perfect investment. The house "will appreciate in value," she thought, "and the proceeds should be enough to provide for my burial costs when the time comes."

The petite 4'11" woman found the four-room, two bedroom house on the smaller front lot the perfect size. It was relatively easy to keep clean, and had a small yard where she planned to install a white picket fence to provide a secure play area for her future great grandchildren. The additional one-plus acre vacant lot behind the house provided the perfect space for a retirement home of her daughter Margie, her son-in-law Paul and their children Matthew and Heather. Building a house on that lot might require minor relief from the zoning code, relief that is generally relatively easy to obtain. If permission was denied, then she would simply build a large addition to the existing house which would be used by her daughter with the smaller house serving as an in-law apartment for her. But, as often happens, the plans changed.

Just months after moving into the small house, she determined that living alone did not suit her. She missed the hustle and bustle of her daughter's house and decided to move back into their home. In an accommodation that seemed to benefit everyone, she sold the small house to her son-in-law who provided a home for his son Matthew and daughter-in-law who was now pregnant with Paul and Margie's first grandson. Over the course of the ensuing years, a combination of the declining Rhode Island real estate market, Matthew's divorce from his wife and a dramatic decrease in Paul's salary led to the home's foreclosure by the bank. Matthew and his family, which by now included three children, joined Paul and Margie in their North Providence home reuniting the entire family under one roof.

With no money left in the bank and her only asset the undeveloped lot on Bishop Hill Road in Johnston, LaCourse once again started to think of her own death and the financial burden that it would place on her family. The now seventy-six year old decided to sell her land as a means of providing for her current and expanding medical needs as well as her future internment expenses. The property was listed with Affiliated Real Estate in 2010 for an asking price of $60,000. The price was below market value, but thought a fair price considering that the buyer may need to incur the expense of appearing before the zoning board for a variance before building on the lot. The next several months saw plenty of interest in the lot, but no offers. Over two years passed without an offer to purchase the property.

During this time, Carol's son-in-law Paul's ninety year-old father passed away, leaving his 88 year-old mother Anna alone in her home. Unwilling to consider nursing home care as an option, a decision was made to have Anna move in with Paul's sister Linda and her family. Linda and Dennis Corsini had been married since 1970 and together they had one son, Michael, who at age 31 lived in the lower portion of the raised ranch with his girlfriend Becky. Their North Providence home, with its one full bath and two bedrooms, was just not big enough for the five people who now occupied it. Linda, Dennis and Michael decided to build a larger house that would be big enough for both the existing family members and any new family additions that time might produce.

After a family meeting, Carol LaCourse decided to sell her land to Michael for the sum of $10,000. Though assessed by the Town of Johnston for $66,000, Carol determined that the $10,000 would provide for her burial and allow Michael to build his new home using the equity in the land as part of the down payment. Prior to applying for the zoning variance that town officials said was required before the issuance of a building permit, however, Michael would need to pay 3 ½ years of property tax arrearage. He also agreed to absorb the $780.00 cost of the application to the Johnston Zoning Board for the variance from the zoning code's 140' frontage requirement. Michael's total financial committment was $9,181.70.

The Johnston town government is run by an elected Mayor and five elected council members. There is an elected school committee and various appointed boards and commissions including the Johnston Zoning Board of Review. While the elected council is responsible for zoning changes, minor variances from, and exceptions to, the Town's Zoning Ordinance are left to this 5-member appointed body. Although variances may be considered minor relative to large-parcel zone changes, they are no less vital to those appearing before the Board as they can have a profound impact on the lives of those who come before it.

Rhode Island general law itself recognizes the significant consequences of a zoning board's decisions and therefore sets very specific legal standards for boards to follow when approving or denying a zoning variance or exception. The criteria that zoning boards must consider when deciding issues of dimensional relief include assurance that the relief sought is due to the unique characteristics of the subject land or structure and not due to the general characteristics of the surrounding area or the physical or economic disability of the petitioner. Likewise, consideration must be given to the cause of the hardship to assure that it is not the result of any prior action of the petitioner and does not result primarily from the desire of the petitioner to realize greater financial gain. Zoning Boards are required to ensure that the granting of the requested variance will not alter the general character of the surrounding area or impair the intent or purpose of the zoning ordinance or the comprehensive plan upon which the ordinance is based, and that the relief to be granted is the least relief necessary. In other words, relief may not be granted to allow for a duplex when a single family home is an option. Finally, the board must determine that the hardship suffered by the owner of the subject property if the dimensional variance is not granted amounts to more than a mere inconvenience.

Not wanting to have the zoning application rejected on some technicality, Paul, acting as a Realtor on behalf of his mother-in-law Carol LaCourse, spoke to his long-time friend Bernie Frezza, the Chairman of the Johnston Zoning Board, seeking advice on the procedure for applying for a variance in Johnston. Though Paul had served on the North Providence Zoning Board of Review for eight years, and the North Providence Town Council for almost seventeen more, he knew that each municipality had its own particular procedure for such applications. Chairman Frezza advised Paul that it sounded like a routine enough request, but instructed him to see the Town's Building Official, Ben Nascenzi, for complete instructions and application forms. Bernie offered to call Ben and ask him to "walk you through" the process and provide everything that would be needed to make the application. Frezza also advised Paul to call Councilwoman Stephanie P. Manzi, the area councilperson, as a courtesy to alert her to the impending application. A former councilman, Paul certainly understood that no elected official enjoys being surprised by residents asking about a project that is completely unfamiliar. He would extend the courtesy to Manzi.

Paul, his nephew Michael Corsini and Michael's girlfriend Becky, met with Nascenzi at the Building and Zoning Office in late April 2013. Nascenzi reviewed the plat map and associated information He noted that the lot lacked adequate frontage and advised the would-be buyer that he would in fact need to complete a zoning application, identify and notify the list of abutters, pay the associated fees, and present his case to the Zoning Board which next "meets on May 30th." He advised that the petitioner retain the services of a registered land surveyor as the application required the submission of a class 1 survey, as well as an attorney who knows how to identify the property abutters that required notification. When asked, he suggested attorney Alfred Russo Jr. and surveyor Nick Veltri as two professionals that have significant experience appearing before the Johnston Zoning Board and can make the process very easy. His suggestion was taken and Russo and Veltri were retained within the next couple of days; Russo at a cost of $1,000 and Veltri, $2,400. Each of these fees were paid by Michael Corsini bringing the gross amount of his investment to $13,361.70. With the information needed to proceed in hand, Caranci was ready to follow Frezza's final piece of advice by calling Councilwoman Manzi and informing her of the impending application in her district. Despite several phone calls, some leaving very specific messages, none were returned.

Veltri did an amazing job accommodating the short application window and the completed zoning application, along with the list of abutters, proof of notification, and the class 1 survey, were submitted to the Town on April 25th for hearing on Thursday May 30, 2013.

Veltri and Russo agreed with Nascenzi's assessment that there was no basis for denial of the application since it met all the criteria necessary for the zoning board's approval and sought the least relief possible to make the land usable – the petitioners simply needed to wait for the hearing.

All that changed during the week of May 23rd, however. Paul Caranci was at work in his office when he received a text message from Bernie Frezza asking if Paul would be at the State House that day. Paul knew that such an urgent message could not be good news and his suspicions were confirmed in a phone conversation when Bernie told him there was a problem with the application. It seems that one of the neighbors, in fact the person that purchased from the bank the very house that Paul had lost to foreclosure, was objecting to the granting of the variance. "But there are no grounds for denial," Caranci protested. Frezza said that grounds didn't matter. It was political and the new owner of 19 Bishop Hill Road was none other than Council President Robert Russo. He had informed Mayor Joseph Polisena of his objection and the Mayor made calls to the Board inquiring about the variance. Frezza sounded downhearted and didn't hold out much promise for approval in light of the neighbors objections.

Caranci contacted the Corsinis to tell them of the latest developments and explained the circumstances to attorney Russo. While most realized that the hearing would probably not favor the applicant, the Carancis and Corsinis prepared their case to be presented to the Board.

Several people filed into the Johnston Senior Citizen Center at 1291 Hartford Avenue in Johnston. This was the former site of the once popular El Marocco Club, a fine dining and night club facility of days gone by. Tonight, it was the site of the May 30th meeting of the Johnston Zoning Board. Several cases donned the docket and each went exceedingly well for the applicant ending in approval. Among those present to observe the proceedings was Council President Robert Russo, prompting one attorney who appears at most meetings to say, "Why is Russo here? He never attends these meetings." Paul and his family knew why he was there! The only question they had was whether or not he would offer his own testimony or simply impact the vote by his presence.

Chairman Frezza called the case of Carol LaCourse and Attorney Russo introduced the application reciting all the required points of law. He noted the presence of applicant Michael Corsini, Paul Caranci, his expert real estate witness, and land surveyor, Nick Veltri.

Russo began to describe the project when he was interrupted almost immediately by an incredulous Anthony

Pilozzi. "What were those dimensions again?" Pilozzi asked. "Forty seven by eighty seven, I think," Russo responded. With that, the verbal assault on Russo began essentially derailing any semblance of an ordered hearing on the salient points. Though the footprint of the proposed construction is not one of the criteria on which the Board can decide a case if all front, rear and side lot restrictions are met, the dimensions of the home became the entire focus of questioning by the Board. And the questioning was intense! Russo tried desperately to bring the discussion back to the relevant facts explaining how the variance, if granted, would conform to other properties in the area. "There are two means of ingress and egress to the property," Russo noted. "One is 30'8" wide. It is an easement on the right hand side. The other is 21'9" on the left hand side of the property...Again the code here requires 140' of frontage. If you look at the assessors map Mr. Veltri provided here this evening and look at all of the lots that abut Bishop Hill Road, only three in that vicinity have the required 140'. All of the other properties have less. In fact, some of them have far less."[227]

Pilozzi interrupted again saying that two separate areas of frontage cannot be combined and therefore, the actual frontage of the lot was only 30', not the 52' being alleged. Russo pointed out that zoning law does not require that the areas of frontage be contiguous to be considered part of a lot's frontage, but a belligerent Pilozzi replied, "I see your point, I mean, but I'm not, I'm looking at it a different way. I'm looking at it - I want to interpret the zoning law the way I see it."[228] Caranci glanced at his wife and sister. "Can he be serious?" he thought to himself.

Pilozzi continued saying he thought the 30' ingress would cause a problem for public safety vehicles and endanger the safety and welfare of the neighborhood because at least 50' is required to turn a fire truck around. Russo was unable to get a word in over the excited voice of Pilozzi. Eventually Chairman Frezza asked Veltri if there was enough room for a fire truck to turn around. Veltri pointed out that unlike all the other properties that might require a fire truck to actually turn around, this property has a circular driveway that allows the truck to continue in the same direction to access and egress the property. This testimony rendered Pilozzi's objection moot.

Russo tried to continue with his presentation, but Pilozzi, now joined by the Board's attorney, Joseph Ballirano, kept interrupting with one irrelevant question and/or statement after another. They tried to make an issue out of an easement owned by the petitioner but used by others to access rear land despite its irrelevance to the application being heard. Even the property address noted on the petition became an issue. Vacant land is typically identified by the street number of the closest property since no street number is assigned to vacant lots. In this case 19 Bishop Hill Road, the address of Council President Russo's rental house, was used because it is the house immediately in front of the vacant lot and once owned by Caranci. Pilozzi felt that since there was another Bishop Hill property using the number 19, emergency responders would be confused by this property being identified as such. Russo had to point out that this would not be the number of a new house that was being proposed for development but rather it was simply the number being used on the application to identify the, as yet, unnumbered parcel of land – "a concept that should not be difficult for a zoning professional to grasp, but apparently is!", Caranci thought.

Eventually, discussion turned to an appropriate area of concern, conformance with the neighborhood. Incredibly, Pilozzi turned even that discussion into a joke proclaiming that since the older homes in the area have driveways of between 60' and 100', the proposed development would not conform. Russo countered. "I don't see that Mr. Pilozzi. The lot in question has 55,779 square feet. It is the largest piece of residential property in that neighborhood."[229] Again, he was interrupted with a pointless question and not allowed to continue his thought.

Board member Joseph Anzelone joined the discussion. "[The application] doesn't indicate wetlands, but they think there may be wetlands,"[230] he said. "What in God's name is he talking about?," Caranci thought. "Where would the wetlands be?" Veltri responded that the property has no wetlands. It is basically upland and is surrounded by developed property which would be indicative of property devoid of wetlands. Pilozzi perceived an opening however and pounced noting that the application did not have results from a PERK test (A PERK test determines availability of well water, but this property had town water available to it.) or an ISDS permit (an individual septic design system provides for sewage waste disposal when municipal sewer systems are not available in an area). The inference was that the lack of a PERK test and an ISDS permit might be indicative of wetlands. However, neither the test nor the permit were required as part of the zoning application. A PERK test is not required because the property has access to public water and the ISDS permit is not required because it involves significant engineering work and is therefore quite expensive. Such tests results and permits are typically procured once the building permits have been obtained which is well after the zoning board hearing. Consequently and ISDS permit is rarely sought before zoning approvals are received and seldom included with an application for a zoning variance. Finally, as if the discussion could not get any more absurd or deviate any further from the Board's authority, the members began asking about the number of bedrooms and bathrooms the proposed dwelling would have. Russo again tried to bring the members back to a relevant discussion about the issues at hand, but the session began to degenerate into a one-sided shouting match with Ballirano and Pilozzi clearly showing their bias against the application and exerting intimidation factors to encourage the petitioner's silence. At least that's how the petitioners viewed it!

Testifying as a real estate expert, Paul Caranci noted that the plan is for a single family house, the least relief possible. Board attorney Ballirano interrupted. "This design is least relief necessary as an expert under oath? This design is the least relief that this applicant can ask for? Are you serious?" he screamed. [231] Caranci remained calm responding, "A single-family dwelling..." Ballirano again interrupted him mid-sentence. "Single family use with four bedrooms is the least relief necessary. That is ridiculous!" Caranci continued, "The law defines the least relief as a use of property not the number of bedrooms or bathrooms it might have." "It is the totality of circumstances," Ballirano shot back. [232]

In the end, the Board voted 4-1 to deny the application. Pilozzi put forward an incoherent and irrelevant motion saying, "First of all, it is excessive relief because of the size of the house with this particular plan. I mean the number of bedrooms are excessive for that neighborhood. The number of bathrooms there are going to be a septic system there which we didn't touch on too much, no ISDS permit has been granted by the Department of Environmental Management bring up the question of water which two of the abutters are concerned with. It is just not the site for it. It is a buildable lot. Make that clear for the record. But it is not the site for this particular plan: Four bedrooms. It is just probably going to be a beautiful house. It just does not fit at that site. There is no way it fits in that conformance in that neighborhood. The excessive relief, there is also height relief, they need four feet one of the abutters is also concerned with that. Now to go into, it doesn't – there is an adverse impact on the neighborhood with a house of this size. It is not in conformance with the neighborhood and I don't think it would be more than a mere inconvenience to deny this. I know the Viti doctrine is not in place anymore, but if we were to deny it, it is not more than a mere inconvenience because they have the rightful use of the property. It is a buildable lot. So I will base my findings of fact on what I said this particular plan is just too large for that site. It is not in conformance with the neighborhood, and certainly it is not in conformance with the least relief necessary. It is a huge house and it just doesn't fit there. That is the basis for my motion to deny."[233]

The second for the motion, offered by member Joseph Anzelone was equally strange. In his second, Anzelone offered excerpts from a document that was not even

introduced into the record and one that Caranci and Corsini didn't even know existed. It appears that Town Planner Pamela Sherrill provided a letter to the Zoning Board
recommending approval of the variance because of the applications conformance to the Town's comprehensive plan
and the neighborhood. Incredibly, however, Anzelone
skipped the most salient points and pointed to a solitary
sentence in which Sherrill noted that upon granting of the
variance the petitioner will need to complete an ISDS on
the property to ensure that there are no wetlands. As mentioned earlier, such permits are generally sought after zoning board approval for construction is granted. Yet, as if not
wanting to leave the issue alone, Pilozzi tried to infer that
the lot may contain wetlands paraphrasing a very select
sentence of the Town Planner's letter suggesting that further site evaluation be done because of the slope of the
property. Neither Anzelone nor Pilozzi ever bothered to
note that the Town Planner had acknowledged conformance and recommended approval. The actual letter reads,
"The proposed single family residence with public water
and private OWTS appears to be consistent with the Town
of Johnston Comprehensive Community Plan, including
the following practices: Policy LU-7b Encourage compati-
ble infill developments that are scaled and designed to fit
their surroundings in the urbanized area. Policy LU-8b
Achieve a harmonious relationship between residential
land use patterns, non-residential uses, and the natural
landscape in order to preserve the Town's environmental
resources for the benefit and enjoyment of present and future generations."[234]

The letter concludes, "The proposed infill development would be consistent with the character of the single

family neighborhood and therefore would be consistent with the comprehensive plan."[235]

At the conclusion of the meeting, attorney Ballirano approached Caranci who was talking with his family members, and offered an apology saying, "Sorry about all this. You'll win this in court."

The petitioners retained the services of the Law Offices of Michael Kelly, PC to file the appeal. Attorney John Mancini explained the process noting that an appeal of this type can take anywhere from 12-24 months to go through the courts and it isn't cheap. He required a $5,000 retainer noting that if the cost exceeded that, the balance would be due as the costs were incurred. The LaCourse, Caranci and Corsini families discussed the options. With the advancing age of the two mothers, time was certainly a concern and the potential cost was equally concerning. But it was felt that there wasn't a choice. Not appealing would render the land unusable, unsaleable, and essentially worthless. There was far more to lose by doing nothing. The decision was made!

On November 6, 2013 LaCourse filed with the Rhode Island Superior Court a memorandum of law in support of her appeal. In hearing such appeals "the court shall not substitute its judgment for that of the zoning board of review as to the weight of the evidence on questions of fact. The court may affirm the decision of the zoning board of review or remand the case for further proceedings, or may reverse or modify the decision if substantial rights of the appellant have been prejudiced because of findings, inferences, conclusions, or decisions which are:

1. In violation of constitutional, statutory, or ordinance provisions;
2. In excess of the authority granted to the zoning board of review by statute or ordinance;
3. Made upon unlawful procedure;
4. Affected by other error of law;
5. Clearly erroneous in view of the reliable, probative, and substantial evidence of the whole record; or
6. Arbitrary or capricious or characterized by abuse of discretion or clearly unwarranted exercise of discretion."[236]

This judicial review must be measured against the zoning board's obligation under the law in reviewing applications for dimensional relief. The criteria are spelled out in the town's zoning code and are five in number. First, the board must ensure "that the hardship from which the plaintiff seeks relief is due to the unique characteristics of the subject land or structure and not due to a physical or economic disability of the plaintiff." Second, "that the hardship is not the result of any prior actions of the plaintiff and does not result primarily from the desire of the plaintiff to realize greater financial gain." Third, "that the granting of the requested variance will not alter the general character of the surrounding area or impair the intent or purpose of the zoning ordinance or the comprehensive plan upon which the ordinance is based. Fourth, "that the relief to be granted is the least relief necessary," and fifth, "that the hardship suffered by the owner of the subject property if the dimensional variance is not granted amounts to more than a mere inconvenience.[237]

Clearly, the memorandum points out citing relevant case law, the petitioner met that burden leaving the zoning board no choice under the law but to grant the petitioner's request. The memorandum continues, "…the Board's decision is in violation of constitutional provisions in that it operates as a taking of the Appellant's Property…The Board's decision prevents the Appellant from constructing any type of home on the Property, if she is required to seek relief as to frontage, as she was required as part of the Application. This prevents the beneficial use of the Property, as the Appellant would not be able to construct a home, which is permitted by right, in her R-40 zone, despite having the requisite lot area to do so, and despite having paid taxes on such a 'buildable lot,' as the Board deemed it to be. Even Board member Frezza recognized that: 'I hope you realize that something is going to go there. They have a right to put a house in there.' " The memorandum also describes the Board's decision as "an excess of its authority" in that it "improperly focused on the use of the property, which was permitted, and not the dimensional relief requested." The memorandum rightfully notes that "throughout the entire hearing, and in its decision, the Board improperly focused on the use of the property, which is a permitted use" in the zone. "In fact, the Board, through his Solicitor, who testified and spoke on the application on numerous occasions throughout the hearing specifically stated that: 'The concerns so far with the application are not the lots. It's the use that you are proposing with that specific plan….' "238

Finally, the memorandum alleges that "the Board's temperament and decision were politically motivated and an abuse of discretion." In support of that claim the petitioner points to the complete meeting transcript which "reveals troublesome treatment of the Applicants by the Zoning Board members and its counsel" because "Councilman Robert Russo is a direct abutter to the Property, owning, in part, lot 99." The memorandum further alleges that "the Board had a predisposition towards the application and did not consider the application in a fair and impartial manner as is required by any quasi-judicial board."[239]

The cost of situational political corruption is clear. The active corruption of those zoning board members who voted to deny the petition for reasons thought to be political, and the passive corruption of those members who were not part of that decision but supported the motion to deny for some unknown reason, possibly even out of fear of offending another politician, had a profound negative impact on three families. The Corsini's continued to live in cramped quarters until Michael purchased a new home for himself and Becky. LaCourse failed to receive proceeds of the sale of the land leaving her to struggle with her monthly medical payments and property tax payments for an additional two years. She invested another $7,000 into the cost of the appeal. All totaled, LaCourse spent an additional $10,000 of borrowed money that will never be recouped.

On April 11, 2014, RI Superior Court Associate Justice Brian VanCouyghen issued his ruling vacating the decision of the Johnston Zoning Board. Rather than focus its attention on the merits of the case presented, however, the Court narrowed its attention to procedure noting, "This court finds that the notice provided to the public was inadequate because it failed to describe 'the precise character of the relief sought' by the Appellant. In particular, the notice failed to mention that Appellant was seeking dimensional relief from the height requirements of the ordinance."[240] Because the height relief was distinctly requested by the Appellant and part of the Board's decision to deny relief, the Court viewed the Town's omission as inadequate public notice. This fatal flaw in the filing meant that the Board did not have the authority to act. The failure to provide proper notice, the Court ruled, renders the Board's decision a nullity creating a situation that relieved the Court of its obligation to address the merits of the appeal.

The original zoning application submitted to the Town of Johnston by Nick Veltri on behalf of the petitioner clearly requests relief from both frontage and height requirements. Once received, the Town failed to advertise it properly yet, the Zoning Board members discussed both forms of requested relief at the hearing creating the condition that led to the Court's decision. Because the Court ruled that the discussion of height relief shouldn't have taken place, it nullified the meeting. LaCourse, to gain the required relief, would have no alternative but to begin the entire process again, filing an application for a new zoning board hearing. The cost and time involved in doing that with no guarantee of a different outcome, and having already lost the potential buyer, were prohibitive and LaCourse decided instead to relist the property for sale subject to the potential buyer obtaining any necessary permits.

As if to add insult to injury, the attorney that handled the Zoning Board appeal in Superior Court advised LaCourse that there was no need to appeal to the Zoning Board for the frontage because it was a pre-existing condition that was not being extended by any action of the property owner. In fact, she said, the Johnston Building Official should have advised the buyer of that fact and issued the permit in the first place.

A purchase and sales agreement to sell the land to a speculative investor was signed in December 2014. The sales price was 50% below the assessed value because the developer feared what the Town of Johnston may require of the developer before allowing construction on the site.

As it turned out, that investor obtained a building permit from the Johnston Building Official to build a house similar to the one proposed by Michael Corsini, albeit a little smaller. The developer obtained the permit without the intervention of the Zoning Board and without the objection of the same Town Building Official who had previously informed Corsini that Zoning Board relief would absolutely be required. The closing of escrow was held in April 2015 a full two years after the original application for a zoning board hearing was submitted by LaCourse.

Later in that same year Ben Nascenzi was accused of racism in delaying the issuance of building permits in a case in which the facts seemed eerily familiar. On November 24, 2015, GoLocalProv.com posted a video in which Nascenzi was "heard making a racially charged statement regarding a church pastor's attempts to rehabilitate a historic church in town. In an expletive-laden phone conversation with his supervisor and the contractor on the project that was taped, Johnston Building Inspector Ben Nascenzi can be heard referring to Reverend Dr. Chris Abhulime as 'the fucking black owner' of the former historic Belknap Church." Abhulime told GoLocal that since purchasing the building on 500 Greenville Avenue in Johnston this past spring, that he has been stopped in his attempts to rehabilitate the property." Abhulime explained that after he decided to purchase the property, "which had been used as a church for a hundred years, we were then subject to zoning approval. So then we applied for zoning to use it for a church – we had an attorney and surveyor, we submitted the application, and they gave us an appointment for June 25th. We paid the fees, the attorney, the surveyor. At the meeting, there appeared to be plenty of time, there were people ahead of us - had good conversation with the zoning officials, so when it came our time, it didn't seem like there'd be an issue. But then it became obvious they were going to deny us. It only lasted 4-5 minutes, and they didn't tell us why it was denied. Most of what they said was, 'Are you done, are you done? That is not how a zoning hearing should be held. We paid quite a lot just to get dismissed within five minutes,"Abhulime said.

Abhulime explained that there is an appeal in RI Superior Court, "so we went ahead and purchased it." After informing his parishioners of the purchase, several drove to Johnston to check out the building. A couple of days later, Abhulime said he received a call from Nascenzi asking "why I brought so many cars, so many black people, and said he authorized the police to act if we went back."
The inspector, according to Abhulime, accused the Pastor of holding a service at the church, something Abhulime denies. "They couldn't get rid of us through zoning," the pastor said, "now they're making it hard," Abhulime concluded.

Regardless of the outcome of this case which is still ongoing, the allegations demonstrate the impact that unfettered power can have and how, once situational corrup

Bishop Hill House - front and rear view and ready for sale.

tion is allowed to flourish and take root, it strengthens and becomes a force almost too powerful for the average citizen to overcome.

The cost of situational corruption, both active and passive as described in this story, is high. The actions of the Johnston Zoning Board, potentially motivated by a desire to appease a community leader at the expense of the citizens the board members are appointed to serve, are not unique. Similar scenarios are repeated in countless political jurisdictions throughout the United States almost on a daily basis. Only when those elected and appointed officials understand that such politically motivated actions do in fact constitute corrupt deeds, will there be any hope of a criminal judicial redress of active and passive situational political corruption.

7

POLITICIANS PROTECTING THEIR OWN

The Brian Quirk Story

Police departments are established in jurisdictions throughout the United States for the protection of its citizens from the actions of those who would benefit from violating the laws. Most of us expect that when we call the police to report a crime, harassment or some other unlawful activity, the end result will be the administration of justice. At least that's the expectation. But what happens when the violator is an elected official who enjoys the protection of high ranking public officials and the police in the cover-up of his actions?

Brian Quirk moved from Watertown, Massachusetts to a quiet North Providence, Rhode Island neighborhood toward the end of 1986. Brian and his wife Sharon loved their new home and began to raise their family which grew to include two sons. After almost 20 years in North Providence, however, Brian and his family became the target of, what Brian termed, systematic harassment and relentless and unjustified vengeance at the hands of a couple of neighbors with a personal ax to grind. He turned to law enforcement for help only to uncover an alleged web of deceit and collusion resulting from a perverted sense of camaraderie between the harassers and some key town officials. Those relationships obstructed any attempt for the Quirk family to obtain justice. What followed over the next 9 years is nothing short of extraordinary.

Brian Quirk

During the fall of 2005, the Quirk's received word that Brian's father, who along with his wife, had retired to Falmouth, MA, had terminal cancer. Treating and caring for him in Rhode Island required that the Quirks invite Brian's parents to join his family in their North Providence home. To accommodate the expanded family, the Quirks now needed more living space, but didn't want to leave their neighborhood. By coincidence, the larger house right next door to the Quirk's home was listed for sale. The Quirks inquired of the Realtor and learned that the owner was negotiating with two parties that were deadlocked with prices substantially less than the asking price. The Quirk's responded by submitting a bid offering the full price of $329,999.00. Eventually, one of the other parties, relatives of the Quirk's neighbors, purchased the home for the much higher price, but they apparently blamed the Quirks for driving up the cost.

Still without any prospects of a new home by spring 2006, the Quirks made a decision to simply build an addition on their existing home in order to provide the space necessary to accommodate Brian's parents. The Quirks hired a contractor and decided to make a photo album chronicling the various stages of construction. While taking pictures of the improvements, Brian had his first run-in with another neighbor, Joseph Giammarco, a state worker. An irate, and perhaps guilt-ridden Giammarco, accused Quirk of taking pictures of him while he was using a RI Department of Transportation vehicle to transport trees and shrubs to his home, something he probably should not have been doing,[241] according to Quirk.

These two unrelated incidents led to the formation of an alliance between the two neighbors determined to unleash the most heinous and cowardly acts of harassment and torment against the Quirks throughout the last few months of Brian's father's life and beyond. As Brian explained to the North Providence Town Council both verbally and through the submission of detailed official documents, the neighbors' actions, "spawned by vindictiveness and the aid of certain town officials," gave the neighbors cause for delight.[242]

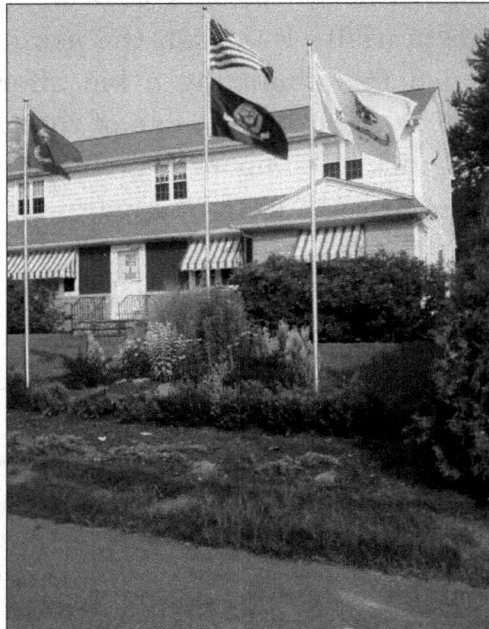

Brian Quirk and his wife Sharon raised their family and cared for Brian's elderly parents in this Norrth Providence home.

It started in March of 2006 with late night harassing phone calls in which the caller would not speak. On April 20th however, during one of a string of harassing phone calls, the caller left a message accusing Quirk of "not being

man enough to speak with him" and threatening to "run
[them] out of the neighborhood and burn down the house."

Dear Resident,

It has been an honor to serve you as your District 2 Town Councilman during the past 4 years. During my tenure on the council I have focused my efforts on restoring fiscal health to the Town by supporting realistic budgets and budget cuts that have trimmed the size of government. The reduction in the size of municipal government has eliminated waste without compromising the high level of services that our residents expect.

As a longtime resident, I have worked tirelessly to increase the quality of life for all of our residents. I strongly supported the acquisition of Camp Meehan, sponsored annual town clean up days, and implemented a Town beautification plan over the last two years that included planting trees at the towns library, schools and along Mineral Spring Avenue at no expense to the taxpayers. I recently lobbied for and received a grant from RIPTA that funded placing trash barrels at all bus stops. I respectfully ask for your support on September 11, 2012. I will continue to support financial decisions that continue to stabilize the Town's financial future and tax base and which in turn increase the quality of life for the residents of North Providence.

Sincerely,
Joseph Giammarco

Joseph Jr., Inga (dog), Joe, Kathy

Joe Giammarco
Vote September 11, 2012
Endorsed Democrat Town Council District 2
Paid for by Friends of Giammarco.

*Joe Jr., dog Inga, Joe Giammarco, and Kathy
from a 2012 campaign flyer used by Giammarco
during his campaign for town council.*

The caller also left his name; Joe Giammarco.[243] This threat proved to the Quirks that Giammarco was confrontational, irrational and dangerous and prompted the first incident report taken by the North Providence Police who listened to the message. By May 25th, Giammarco's threats against the Quirks took on new meaning as both of the Quirks vehicles were damaged while parked outside their home in apparent retaliation for Quirk calling the police.[244] Just three weeks later, the Quirk's awakened to find that the tires on both their vehicles had been slashed overnight. The damaged tires were replaced only to be slashed again the following night.[245]

Giammarco meanwhile, was having problems in his own family. Giammarco had been drinking again, and his wife had had enough. On July 23, 2006, when his wife and son failed to come home, Giammarco filed a missing person report with the North Providence Police. The police eventually located the missing pair who acknowledged that "they were fine, but had had it with his [Joe Giammarco's] drinking."[246]

North Providence Police Department   Page: 1
NARRATIVE FOR PATROL OFFICER CHRISTOPHER E DYSON   08/10/2007

Ref: 06-2585-OF

On 09/30/06 I was dispatched to 6 Amelia Court in reference to a suspicious noise. Upon arrival I spoke with resident Brian Quirk 07/12/57 DOB. Mr. Quirk at this time stated he heard something strike the rear of his residence. Upon going outside, he observed his neighbor Joseph Giammarco ▮▮▮▮ DOB , walking across the street , and into his garage at ▮ Oak Knoll Court.

Mr. Quirk at this time checked the rear of his residence and located a piece of 2x3 on the lawn and further stated the police have been called to his residence on more than one occasion in regards to Mr. Giammarco. Upon picking up the wood, a lumber tag was observed as follows: Irving 2x3, bar code # 98945 06006 7.

At this time I responded to ▮ Oak Knoll Court to speak with Mr. Giammarco. Upon arrival Mr. Giammarco was standing in the garage, at his feet was a power mitre box covered in saw dust, a large amount of saw dust in the driveway, and a small pile of lumber in the driveway as well. While speaking with Mr. Giammarco and his brother, Armand Giammarco ▮▮▮▮ DOB, I asked Joseph if he was familiar with the piece of wood I located at 6 Amelia Court. At which time he stated no and further stated that he has had problems with that party in the past.

While looking at the pile of lumber in the driveway, I also observed a Irving lumber tag on one of the pieces. Upon picking it up, it was marked identically with the exact bar code as the piece located on Amelia Court. Mr. Giammarco at this time was advised not to have any contact with Mr. Quirk and was advised not to trespass on the Quirk property.

Upon advising Mr. Quirk of the above investigation, he stated he would be obtaining a restraining order against Mr. Giammarco. No damage was visible on Mr. Quirk's property at this time. Both pieces of wood were confiscated and marked where located. Both items were tagged and placed into temporary evidence.

The police report of 8-10-2007 led to the arrest of Giammarco.

The following month, the police arrived at the home of Brian Quirk informing him that, as the result of an anonymous complaint, he would have to remove his son's basketball hoop which violated the Town's ordinance. Despite the existance of hundreds of similar hoops scattered at other homes throughout the Town, the Quirks complied. [247]

Around the same time, the Quirks began receiving late night pizza deliveries to their home, pizza that they never ordered! On September 8th, Giammarco, who was now a candidate for the North Providence Town Council, again threatened Quirk, this time yelling at Brian for parking his car on the street outside Quirks home which Giammarco considered to be too close to his home. "I told you not to park there," Giammarco screamed, "I guess you didn't learn your lesson," an obvious reference, Quirk believed, to the slashed tires. "When I'm elected, I'm running you and your family out of town."[248] Giammarco wasn't elected, however, as he failed to garner enough votes to win the September primary.

Toward the end of that month, after retiring to bed for the evening, the Quirk family was awakened by several loud explosion type bangs. Startled, they immediately vacated the premises as a safety precaution. While outside, Quirk caught a glimpse of Giammarco leaving the yard of an abutting neighbor's property and immediately called the police. Upon arriving on the scene, police discovered that several pieces of cut lumber (2 X 3s) had been thrown against Quirk's house. Unfortunately for Giammarco, the pieces still had the store bar codes attached and police were quickly able to match them to similar pieces of cut lumber by matching bar codes on the wood piled up in Giammarco's yard. Police also discovered a power miter saw covered in fresh saw dust.[249]

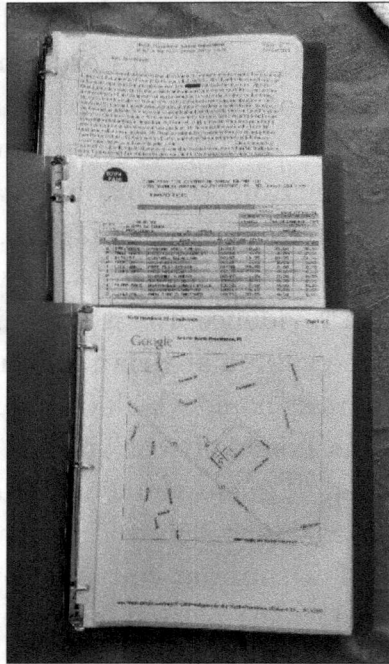

Three volumes of evidence submitted to the town council

On October 19, 2006, Giammarco was arrested by the North Providence Police for his actions against the Quirks.[250] What happened next, according to Brian Quirk, was both shocking and appalling! Captain Joseph Sanita assured the Quirks that the police prosecutor would follow through with a court hearing and there was no longer any need for the Quirks to worry. Neither, he advised, would it be necessary for the Quirks to appear at the court hearing as the police prosecutor would handle the matter. However, on January 4, 2007, the North Providence Police prosecutor failed to attend the criminal hearing resulting in the dismissal of the case under rule 48(a). The Quirks were not only denied the promised justice in this matter, but later learned that Captain Sanita grew up with Giammarco. This fact was learned, however, some years later, only after

Sanita was himself arrested for stealing items from the police department's evidence room.[251]

On December 3, 2006 Quirk, walking to his car, discovered three inch masonry nails strewn across his driveway, and the harassment continued. Throughout the spring and summer of 2007 Quirk received regular visits from town Building Inspector William Signoriello regarding several "egregious" ordinance violations. Each of the visits was attributed to an anonymous complaint. The "egregious" violations included grass that was too long, planting shrubs and flowers without a permit, the improper location of trash cans, renting rooms to strangers, who were actually Quirk's parents, and an illegal flagpole and garden in the backyard. Each time the town official refused to document the visitation or reveal the identity of the complainant.

To the Quirks, the complaints were frivolous, untrue, and not rising to the level of an ordinance violation. They considered these visits just further attempts at harassment and wanted them to stop.

In an effort to put a halt to the unwarranted and unjustified inspections, the Quirks scheduled an appointment with Mayor Charles A. Lombardi, who also serves as the Town's Public Safety Director. Surely, the Quirks believed, the Mayor will be outraged by the activity of his neighbors and the compliant inspectors that seemed to be doing the neighbor's bidding.

But rather than lending a sympathetic ear, the Mayor stunned the Quirks with a pompous display of arrogance. After pleading their case and asking for an end to the harassing visits, Lombardi, who sat back in his oversized chair with his feet on the desk said to the Quirks, "maybe next time you should think about whose sign you put on your front lawn." (a reference to Quirk placing the campaign sign of Lombardi's opponent in his yard during the previous election.)[252]

The Quirks were incredulous at the statement and left the Mayor's office in disgust knowing that they would receive neither satisfaction nor justice from the Town's highest ranking elected official. It was only after Quirk had video cameras installed around his property on July 2nd that future visits from the town's inspectors ceased.

```
            North Providence Police Department          Page: 1
            NARRATIVE FOR PATROLMAN DAVID A TESSERIS      11/14/2007

     Ref: 06-1880-OF

   On 07/23/2006 I was dispatched to ▮ Oak Knoll for a reported missing person. Upon arrival I was met by
Joseph Giammarco▮           Mr. Giammarco stated that on 07/22/2006 at approx. 1045pm his wife Katherine
▮▮▮      and his son Joseph▮▮▮     had left their residence to go purchase vinegar and tomato juice since
their dog had been sprayed by a skunk. They had left using RI registration ▮▮ which is on a 2001 white Ford
Taurus.  Earlier in the night Mr.Giammarco had called the police department to check the Stop & Shop and
Shaws plaza for the vehicle. Those areas were checked and obtained negative results. While speaking with Mr.
Giammarco I had dispatcher 165 send out a BOLO for Katherine and his son while I obtained a statement and
completed missing person reports. While completing these reports I had placed a call to Katherines cell phone
and had left a message for her to call Headquarters then call her residence. I was advised by dispatcher 165 that
Katherine had called HQ looking for me but hung up prior to leaving a message. I then had returned her call on
the cell phone again and left another message. Katherine then had called her husband Joseph on his cell phone
while he was standing in front of me. Joseph stated that she had told them they were fine but had had it with his
drinking. I had no evidence that Joseph had been drinking nor did I have any reason to believe that he had. I then
left another message for Katherine to call me prior to the end of my shift but as of 0615 I have not received a call.
Neither Katherine or Joseph was placed out missing. I asked Mr. Giammarco why his wife would be out driving
around at this hour as opposed to returning home. He replied he had no idea but was very relieved to know that
they were safe. The BOLO was left in the system so if any department came in contact to have her call our HQ
then her residence (check on the well being).
```

Police statement 11-14-2007 regarding the missing person report filed on Giammarco's wife and son who said they let because "they had had it with his drinking."

The very next day, District 2 Councilman Frank Manfredi agreed to try to mediate the situation between Quirk and Giammarco. In fact, Manfredi and his wife did approach Giammarco at a July 4, 2007 fireworks display at the Town's John Notte Park. That effort ended quickly, however, when Giammarco advised Manfredi, "Do not get involved, I want to run the Quirks out of town and after all they are Irish, who wants them around."[253]

On July 31st, the Quirks had a chance encounter with Giammarco who was driving on Mineral Spring Avenue. The Quirks tried to avoid a confrontation, but, according to Brian Quirk, Giammarco seemed determined to create a conflict. After reporting the incident to police, the investigating officer noted in his report that while speaking to Giammarco, the patrolman "smelled an odor of alcohol emanating from his breath."[254] Future police reports taken throughout 2007 and 2008 describe Giammarco's behavior as even more bizarre and irrational, threatening to call the Mayor if the police didn't comply with his demands.[255]

The afternoon of May 15, 2008 was a difficult one for the Quirks. They had spent the day taking Brian's father to several doctors culminating with the news that the elder Quirk would require additional surgery to effectively treat his cancer. Exhausted from the day's events, Brian and his wife Sharon decided to retreat to their backyard to discuss what needed to be done to make Brian's father as comfortable as possible. That's when the heckling started from just over the bushes separating Quirk's back yard from that of the new neighbors. There, Quirk observed Giammarco drinking with members of the neighbor's family and together, they shouted lewd and insulting remarks directed toward Sharon. By this time, the police had already warned Quirk that he could be arrested if he continued to call to them, but feeling worn out and desperate, he dialed the phone anyway. While he was on the phone with police, Giammarco ran to his house and returned to the neighbor's yard with a tiki torch in hand. Giammarco and his neighbor wedged the torch between the bushes and the fence that formed the privacy barrier between the two yards and ignited it. When police arrived, Giammarco removed the torch and held it in his hand away from the fence. After surveying the situation, the police officer informed Quirk that it was not a police matter, but rather a matter that should be handled by the fire department. Almost as soon as the police left Giammarco replaced the torch against the fence again prompting Quirk's call to the fire department. Firemen responded and took a report. Rather than dissuading the neighbors from their continued harassment, however, calling the authorities seemed to intensify Giammarco's harassment techniques. He installed a spotlight and directed the bright beam directly into Brian's father's bedroom window every night.[256] Pushed to the limit, Quirk obtained a restraining order in Superior Court.[257] The restraining order was delivered to Giammarco on May 30th and Quirk thought he might finally enjoy a peaceful summer in his own backyard. Any thoughts of peace that might have flittered through Quirks' mind, however, were soon dispelled as, according to Quirk, the other neighbor, learning of the restraining order against Giammarco, decided to pick up the mantle of harassment against the Quirks while his friend's hands were bound by the court.

That neighbor, while publicly drinking and parading back and forth in front of Quirk's home, became outraged, shouted obscenities and made inappropriate hand gestures. On a rather ongoing basis, he and his extended family members began parking their cars in front and on the side of Quirk's home creating a difficult situation for emergency vehicles that occasionally responded to Quirk's father's medical needs. It became quite clear to the Quirks that that neighbor had been an accomplice of Giammarco's all along as they quickly became the new source of malicious acts and erroneous and anonymous complaints to various town departments against the Quirks.[258]

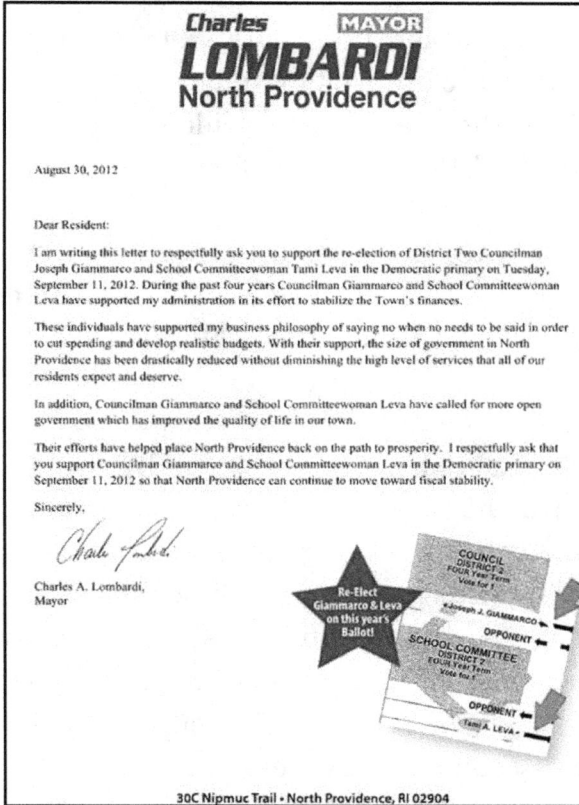

Letter from Charles Lombardi to residents of council district 2 expressing support of Joe Giammarco

As soon as Giammarco was ordered to remove the spotlight that he shone into Quirk's father's bedroom window, the neighbor rigged his lights to shine directly on the Quirk home. Each week that same neighbor placed his trash barrels on either side of the Quirk property and installed professional sized speakers by the side of Quirk's house, frequently blasting them and disrupting any chance of peace and quiet that the Quirk family, including his elderly and sick father, desired. Many times, the neighbor allowed his power lawn mower to run, unattended, by the side window of Quirk's house and the neighbor and his family strategically parked their cars in front and behind of Quirk's vehicles so closely as to render Quirk's vehicles undrivable. All of these actions coincided with the rapid decline of Brian's father's health further exacerbating the Quirks frustration.[259]

On June 16, 2008, police were dispatched to the Quirk home based still again on a frivolous and erroneous complaint filed by the neighbor. Quirk spoke to the responding officer explaining the long-standing issues that existed between the neighbors and expressed his willingness to oblige Lt. Pelagio's request to discuss and resolve all issues with the neighbor's family, but Lt. Pelagio's report concluded that the "neighbors were adamantly unreceptive."[260] The situation quickly worsened when on July 6, 2008, the neighbor deliberately positioned his swimming pool discharge hose under his fence, jetting water into Brian Quirk's son's lower level bedroom window. The young Quirk's computer and desk were ruined.[261] In addition to the photographic evidence collected by Quirk to substantiate the hateful and destructive actions of his neighbor, other impartial neighbors submitted testimony describing the offending neighbors' actions. Yet, nothing came of the incident.

Toward the end of July, the visits to the Quirk residence by the Department of Zoning and Planning commenced, again, based on anonymous complaints. The result was the forced removal of the underground sprinkler system and water drain pipes located on Quirk's property. The town officials reasoned that the underground system extended to close to the unpaved town owned "sidewalk" that was grassed over and maintained by the Quirks. Despite the great number of other residents that have such systems on "town owned" land, only the Quirks were forced to remove their sprinklers and underground water collection system. In an effort to stop the torment that was making Brian's father's last days very uncomfortable, the Quirks filed a court action against the neighbors. In August, 2008, a restraining order was sought but on October 8th, with the elder Quirk's life drawing to an end, a dismissal stipulation was signed.[262]

Brian's father lost his battle with cancer, passing at Brian's home on Sunday October 12, 2008. The elder Quirk's death didn't provide pause to the harassment, however, as in November Joseph Giammarco finally did win election to the North Providence Town Council. The victory was followed, almost immediately by a new notice of violation being issued by the Town's Zoning Officer on the Quirks for "the open lot storage of refuse and rubbish."[263]

In early July, 2009, approximately six months after assuming his seat on the Town Council, Giammarco filed a police report against Brian Quirk for throwing a rock at Giammarco's truck as the two passed each other on the road. Police questioned the Quirks who informed the officers that they were both at home when the incident was alleged to have happened. Police investigated the matter further, speaking with business owners and employees of the businesses located in the vicinity of where the incident had allegedly taken place. Despite their efforts, they were unable to verify anything Giammarco had alleged in his filing.

Quirk responded by delivering a letter to Police Chief John Whiting informing him that Councilman Giammarco had filed a false police report accusing Quirk of throwing a rock at Giammarco's truck and offering unequivocal proof and statements from impartial witnesses disproving Giammarco's accusations. Chief Whiting, however, seemed unimpressed and did nothing in response to Quirk's allegations. (Chief Whiting was later convicted of felonious activity in an unrelated matter and was sentenced to prison. He served several months at the Adult Correctional Institution in Cranston before being released on probation. Giammarco eventually lost his bid for reelection to the town council and the neighbor separated from his wife for a period of time moving out of his North Providence home and living elsewhere.)

During the neighbor's absence from the neighborhood (August 2009 to June 2013), things quieted down for the Quirks. But once the neighbor returned, he resumed his role as instigator and began provoking fights as well as once again placing anonymous complaints to the Division of Inspections. In addition to this juvenile behavior, the neighbor actually challenged Quirk to a fight.[264] After receiving several of these challenges, Quirk met with the new North Providence Police Chief, Paul Martellini and Deputy Chief Pelagio to discuss the issue. In an attempt to defuse the issue so as to avoid any further problems, it was decided that a police vehicle would periodically patrol the neighborhood. It was further decided that the police would send Sgt. Perez to Laporchio's house to intervene in the matter if the problems persisted. Once relieved of the corrupt influences that infiltrated the North Providence Police

Department, things seemed to quiet down for the Quirks and the harassment ceased.

B2   Friday, January 9, 2009   RHODE ISLAND

N. Providence councilor arraigned

Joseph J. Giammarco, who pleaded innocent to drunken driving, was arrested after an incident last month during a snowstorm.

BY RICHAR. ' **DUJARDIN**
JOURNAL STAFF WRITER

PROVIDENCE — Newly elected North Providence Councilman Joseph J. Giammarco pleaded innocent to a charge of drunken driving at his arraignment yesterday in District Court.

Giammarco said that, on the advice of his lawyer, he is withholding public comment until his case goes to trial.

Judge Michael A. Higgins set a pretrial conference for Jan. 22 and released Giammarco on $1,000 personal recognizance.

The charge of driving under the influence stems from an incident during a snowstorm the night of Dec. 19. According to police reports, officers responded to a call that there were vehicles in the road on Obed Avenue obstructing snow-removal equipment.

Officer Michael Zaccagnini said that when he arrived, he saw some cars in the middle of the road and he was advised by a woman that she and other residents had moved out into the street to allow a plow to clear their parking lot.

She said that while she waited a man in a white Taurus — later identified as Giammarco — approached and said, "These cars need to be moved right now because the plow truck is one street away and if they're not gone, they will be towed."

The plow operator said he was also approached by Giammarco, who said, "I'm Joe Giammarco, the councilman here. I want these cars towed and the streets cleaned right away."

Zaccagnini said he didn't know who Giammarco was, and after spotting the white Taurus on Charles Street, he radioed the dispatcher to ask if he was a town employee. The dispatcher told him to speak with Mayor Charles Lombardi, who was at the public-works garage monitoring the town's snow-removal operations.

Sergeants Richard J. Varan and Joseph R. Charette pulled Giammarco over on Mineral Spring Avenue to inquire what he was doing on Obed Avenue. The

THE PROVIDENCE JOURNAL / GRETCHEN ERTL

North Providence Councilman Joseph Giammarco, left, appears at his arraignment yesterday in District Court.

officers said they noticed Giammarco, who was then a councilman-elect, leaning against his car as if for support and asked him to take a field sobriety test, which they said he failed. They reported seizing a nearly empty bottle of brandy from beneath the seat of his car.

A maintenance technician with the state Department of Transportation, the 47-year-old Giammarco tried unsuccessfully three times before defeating former interim Mayor John Sisto Jr. by 51 votes in September's Democratic primary. He and other newly elected officials were sworn in on Sunday.

rdujardi@projo.com / (401) 277-7384

The Providence Journal *reporting on the arraignment of Councilman Joseph Giammarco.*

Many neighbors in communities throughout the United States experience problems often resulting in official municipal government intervention. Most often, these situations have a way of working themselves out. Occasionally, however, the incidents will result in the physical harm of one or more of the neighbors. Many newspaper headlines describe how one neighbor killed another over what in retrospect seemed like a meaningless issue. Yet, the situation like the one experienced by the Quirks was not quieted by the authorities, but rather aided and abetted by a couple of corrupt police officers and other town officials that are supposed to exist for the protection of the residents living within their jurisdictional boundaries. A councilman using the police department and the zoning officer as political weapons in an arsenal of hatred and deception can be defined as nothing less than corruption. The actions of the town's public safety director more interested in retribution for a lack of political support than forcing his departments to administer justice further exacerbated the situation. When those actions are ignored or covered up by the actions or inactions of other corrupt officials, the entire system of government begins to break down causing harm and inflicting pain on the very people that those officials are elected and appointed to serve and protect. The Quirk saga provides a graphic example of both active and passive situational corruption and demonstrates the harm that it perpetrates on its victims.

CONCLUSION

Corruption is not always easily recognized and, for years, it has eluded definition. This book has taken the various forms of corruption and placed them into three categories; traditional, circumstantial and situational. Further, it determined that each of those categories of corruption has both an active and a passive component. Despite certain circumstantial and situational acts of corruption not having a criminal component, each has a negative and deteriorating affect, not only on the individual(s) that fall victim to the corrupt acts but to society as a whole.

When an otherwise law abiding citizen falls prey to government corruption in any of its forms, an entire community begins to distrust government. Police are no longer viewed as impartial protectors of society and quasi-judicial bodies can no longer be seen as a place for the administration of justice. In many cases residents may decide to circumvent the proper channels of government choosing instead to take matters into their own hands. Additions may be built on houses without seeking the proper permits, or other actions may be taken without benefit of proper authority for fear that such permission would be unjustly denied. Nothing good can result from such citizen defiance of government, but one might understand how someone could be driven to act that way.

Exacerbating the problem are two totally separate issues that produce the same result. The first is complacency, a refusal to expose these actions for the corrupt deeds that they are. The second is acceptance, and this is perhaps the biggest problem when it comes to bringing an end to government corruption.

Too many people in the United States accept corruption as an enduring part of the day to day government business – perhaps even as an unchanging character flaw of human nature. After the arrest of three sitting councilmen in the Town of North Providence for shaking down legitimate businesses for the payment of bribes in exchange for the fair consideration of the permits they were seeking, one resident told a reporter that she didn't see the need for all the fuss. After all, the three guilty councilmen were not hurting anyone, they were simply enriching themselves. This kind of attitude is dangerous and fosters the continuance of political and governmental corruption at all levels of government. The fact is that corruption of any kind is harmful to every citizen, even those who aren't aware of its existence.

Until all residents unite in their opposition to, and the exposing of, ALL government corruption, nothing will change and our government of the people, by the people and for the people will continue to hurt the people it was intended to help.

NOTES

Notes to the Introduction

[1] Horvitz, Leslie Alan, Corruption Reaches Fork In The Rhode – Political Corruption In Rhode Island, (News World Communications, Inc., 1993 The Gale Group, 2004)

[2] Lanza, Steven P. Executive Editor of the Connecticut Economic Quarterly, Winter 2004 Issue, February 24, 2004; (Connecticut Center For Economic Analysis, University of Connecticut)

[3] Ibid

Notes to Chapter 1 – Bugs in City Hall: Pawtucket Mayor Brian Sarault

[4] Hill, John., November 28, 1999: Public Trust in Police and Politics is Shaken by Scandals (*The Providence Journal*. Providence, RI)

[5] Freeman, Scott and Malinowski, W. Zachary, August 18, 1991: Behind The Charm, Known For His Fancy Tastes as a Kid, Sarault's Political Ascent Was Unfazed by His Grownup Financial Dealings, Part 1 of 2 parts (*The Providence Journal*, Providence, RI)

[6] Ibid

[7] Freeman, Scott and Malinowski, W. Zachary, August 18, 1991: Behind The Charm, Known For His Fancy Tastes as a Kid, Sarault's Political Ascent Was Unfazed by His Grownup Financial Dealings, Part 2 of 2 parts (*The Providence Journal*, Providence, RI)

[8] Ibid

[9] Ibid

[10] Rakowsky, Judy, June 13, 1991: Pawtucket's Sarault Faces Extortion, Mail Fraud Charges; Mayor Arrested in His Office by FBI Agents (*The Providence Journal*, Providence, RI)

[11] Ibid

[12] Mooney, Tom, June 14, 1991: Offer Left Weygand "Speechless" (*The Providence Journal*, Providence, RI)

[13] Ibid

[14] Rakowsky, Judy, June 13, 1991: Pawtucket's Sarault Faces Extortion, Mail Fraud Charges; Mayor Arrested in His Office by FBI Agents (*The Providence Journal*, Providence, RI)

[15] Ibid

[16] Ibid

[17] Malinowski, W. Zachary and Freeman, Scott, October 5, 1991: Grand Jury Indicts Sarault For Third Time. Public Works Director Also Charged. (*The Providence Journal*, Providence, RI)

[18] Ibid

[19] Ibid

[20] Former Mayor Gets 5 ½ Years For Extortion: February 2, 1992 (*The New York Times*, New York)

[21] Castellucci, John, Sarault Says He's Changed Man As He Seeks Mass. Law License: October 16, 2001 (*The Providence Journal*, Providence)

[22] Ibid

[23] Hearing Panel Report, S.J.C. Order Denying Reinstatement Entered By Justice Sosman: July 29, 2002

Notes to Chapter 2 – Real Estate's Not the Only Thing for Sale: Lincoln Town Administrator Jonathon F. Oster
[24] Ziner, Karen Lee, Lincoln Town Administrator Is Charged With Bribery: January 17, 2001 (*The Providence Journal*, Providence)
[25] Ibid
[26] Hill, John, Testimony Centers On $25,000 Payoff: February 6, 2008 (*The Providence Journal*, Providence)
[27] Ibid
[28] Ibid
[29] Ibid
[30] Ibid
[31] Ibid
[32] Ibid
[33] Hill, John, Builder Testifies In Oster Trial: February 7, 2008 (*The Providence Journal*, Providence)
[34] Ibid
[35] Ibid
[36] Ibid
[37] Hill, John, Oster Treatment Of Picerno Described, January 31, 2008 (*The Providence Journal*, Providence)
[38] Ibid
[39] Ibid
[40] Ibid
[41] Hill, John, Oster Tainted Property In Testimony At Oster Trial, February 1, 2008 (*The Providence Journal,* Providence)
[42] Ibid
[43] Ziner, Karen Lee, Lincoln Town Administrator Is Charged With Bribery: January 17, 2001 (*The Providence Journal*, Providence)
[44] Ibid
[45] Hill, John, Former Official's Testimony Heard In Oster Bribery Case: February 8, 2008 (*The Providence Journal*, Providence)
[46] Hill, John, Oster Case Could Wrap Up Next Week: February 16, 2008 (*The Providence Journal*, Providence)
[47] Hill, John, Jury Set To Decide Oster's Bribery Case: February 20, 2008 (*The Providence Journal*, Providence)
[48] Hill, John, Lincoln Official Urged To Resign: February 18, 2002 (*The Providence Journal*, Providence)
[49] Ibid
[50] Ibid
[51] Hill, John, Shocker In Lincoln: February 19, 2002 (*The Providence Journal*, Providence)
[52] Ibid
[53] Hill, John, Legal Moves Made In Bribery Case: November 1, 2007 (*The Providence Journal*, Providence)
[54] Ibid
[55] Hill, John, Jury Set To Decide Oster's Bribery Case: February 20, 2008 (*The Providence Journal*, Providence)
[56] Ibid
[57] Hill, John, Jury Finds Oster Guilty Of Bribery And Extortion Charges: February 22, 2008 (*The Providence Journal*, Providence)
[58] Hill, John, Oster Dead; Apparent Suicide: February 23, 2008 (*The Providence Journal*, Providence)

[59] Hill, John, Counseling Offered To Oster Jury: February 26, 2008 (*The Providence Journal*, Providence)

Notes to Chapter 3: Cash in the Dumpster: Rhode Island Governor Edward DiPrete
[60] Stanton, Mike; Breton, Tracy; Herzog, David; Malinowski, Zachary W., August 9, 1998: Rhode Island on Trial – The story of the case against Edward DiPrete, Part one Chapter 1 The Soldier - Fugitive Banker's Dealings With State Draw Investigators to DiPrete Circle (*The Providence Sunday Journal*. Providence, RI) p. S.01
[61] Ibid
[62] Ibid
[63] Ibid
[64] Ibid
[65] Ibid
[66] Ibid
[67] Ibid
[68] Ibid
[69] Ibid
[70] Ibid
[71] Stanton, Mike; Breton, Tracy; Herzog, David; Malinowski, Zachary W., August 9, 1998: Rhode Island on Trial – The story of the case against Edward DiPrete, Part one Chapter 2 The Parade - Architects and Engineers Swear They Paid to Get State Contracts (*The Providence Sunday Journal*. Providence, RI) p. S.04
[72] Ibid
[73] Ibid
[74] Ibid
[75] Ibid
[76] Ibid
[77] Ibid
[78] Stanton, Mike; Breton, Tracy; Herzog, David; Malinowski, Zachary W., August 9, 1998: Rhode Island on Trial – The story of the case against Edward DiPrete, Part one Chapter 3 Like Birds - With DiPrete's election, Cranston Friend Moves in on Courthouse Renovation (*The Providence Sunday Journal*. Providence, RI) p. S.05
[79] Ibid
[80] Ibid
[81] Ibid
[82] Ibid
[83] Ibid
[84] Ibid
[85] Ibid
[86] Ibid
[87] Ibid
[88] Ibid
[89] Stanton, Mike; Breton, Tracy; Herzog, David; Malinowski, Zachary W., August 9, 1998: Rhode Island on Trial – The story of the case against Edward DiPrete, Part one Chapter 4 Dennis DiPrete's Insiders Portray Governor's Son as Wheeler-Dealer in State Contracts (*The Providence Sunday Journal*. Providence, RI) p. S.08
[90] Ibid
[91] Ibid
[92] Ibid
[93] Ibid, p. 4
[94] Ibid

[95] Stanton, Mike; Breton, Tracy; Herzog, David; Malinowski, Zachary W., August 9, 1998: Rhode Island on Trial – The story of the case against Edward DiPrete, Part one Chapter 5 Big Men on Campus Contractor's Catalog of Payoffs Includes Rigging of Expansion Job at URI Library (*The Providence Sunday Journal*. Providence, RI) p. S.10

[96] Ibid, p 3

[97] Ibid, p. 2

[98] Ibid

[99] Ibid

[100] Ibid

[101] Ibid

[102] Ibid

[103] Ibid

[104] Ibid

[105] Stanton, Mike; Breton, Tracy; Herzog, David; Malinowski, Zachary W., August 9, 1998: Rhode Island on Trial – The story of the case against Edward DiPrete, Part one Chapter 6 Twins - Rodney Brusini Secretly Talks With Prosecutors While Still Employed at Edward DiPrete's Firm (*The Providence Sunday Journal*. Providence, RI) p. S.11

[106] Ibid

[107] Ibid

[108] Ibid

[109] Ibid

[110] Ibid

[111] Ibid

[112] Ibid

[113] Ibid

[114] Ibid

[115] Ibid

[116] Ibid

[117] Ibid

[118] Ibid

[119] Ibid

[120] Ibid

[121] Ibid

[122] Ibid

[123] Ibid

[124] Ibid

[125] Ibid

[126] Ibid

[127] Ibid

[128] Ibid

[129] Ibid

[130] Ibid

[131] Stanton, Mike; Breton, Tracy; Herzog, David; Malinowski, Zachary W., August 9, 1998: Rhode Island on Trial – The story of the case against Edward DiPrete, Part one Chapter 8 Easy Come, Easy Go - Brusini's Accounts of Cash and Trash, Bolster His Hope to Escape Prosecution (*The Providence Sunday Journal*. Providence, RI) p. S.15

[132] Ibid

[133] Ibid

[134] Ibid

[135] Ibid

[136] Ibid

[137] Ibid

[138] Ibid

[139] Ibid

[140] Ibid

[141] Ibid

[142] Ibid

[143] Ibid

[144] Ibid

[145] Stanton, Mike; Breton, Tracy; Herzog, David; Malinowski, Zachary W., August 16, 1998: Rhode Island on Trial – The story of the case against Edward DiPrete, Part two Chapter 9 Million-Dollar Defense In Response to Sweeping Indictments (*The Providence Sunday Journal*. Providence, RI) p. S.01

[146] Ibid

[147] Ibid

[148] Ibid

[149] Ibid

[150] Ibid

[151] Ibid

[152] Ibid

[153] Ibid

[154] Stanton, Mike; Breton, Tracy; Herzog, David; Malinowski, Zachary W., August 16, 1998: Rhode Island on Trial – The story of the case against Edward DiPrete, Part two Chapter 10 Brain and Brawn - New AG Pine Puts Tough Crime Fighter on State's Case Against the DiPretes (*The Providence Sunday Journal*. Providence, RI) p. S.03

[155] Ibid

[156] Ibid

[157] Ibid

[158] Ibid

[159] Stanton, Mike; Breton, Tracy; Herzog, David; Malinowski, Zachary W., August 16, 1998: Rhode Island on Trial – The story of the case against Edward DiPrete, Part two Chapter 11 Turbulence - DiPrete Prosecutor's Career Advances Despite Discipline by Supreme Court (*The Providence Sunday Journal*. Providence, RI) p. S.05

[160] Ibid

[161] Ibid

[162] Ibid

[163] Ibid

[164] Ibid

[165] Ibid

[166] Ibid

[167] Ibid

[168] Stanton, Mike; Breton, Tracy; Herzog, David; Malinowski, Zachary W., August 16, 1998: Rhode Island on Trial – The story of the case against Edward DiPrete, Part two Chapter 12 Thirty More Boxes – DiPretes' Defense Lawyers Suspect Prosecutors May be Holding Back Evidence (*The Providence Sunday Journal*. Providence, RI) p. S.05

[169] Ibid

[170] Ibid

[171] Ibid

[172] Ibid

[173] Ibid

[174] Ibid

[175] Ibid

[176] Stanton, Mike; Breton, Tracy; Herzog, David; Malinowski, Zachary W., August 16, 1998: Rhode Island on Trial – The story of the case against Edward DiPrete, Part two

Chapter 13 Clobbered DiPretes' Lawyers Expose Details of State's Perjury Bargain With Brusini; (*The Providence Sunday Journal*. Providence, RI) p. S.09
[177] Ibid
[178] Ibid
[179] Ibid
[180] Ibid
[181] Ibid
[182] Ibid
[183] Ibid
[184] Stanton, Mike; Breton, Tracy; Herzog, David; Malinowski, Zachary W., August 16, 1998: Rhode Island on Trial – The story of the case against Edward DiPrete, Part two Chapter 14 Stoke of a Pen – DiPrete Case Falters as Judge Declares Wrongdoing by Prosecutors; (*The Providence Sunday Journal*. Providence, RI) p. S. 11
[185] Ibid
[186] Ibid
[187] Ibid
[188] Ibid
[189] Ibid
[190] Stanton, Mike; Breton, Tracy; Herzog, David; Malinowski, Zachary W., August 16, 1998: Rhode Island on Trial – The story of the case against Edward DiPrete, Part two Chapter 15 Teachings - Through Turmoil and Tragedy, the State's Case Moves Ahead (*The Providence Sunday Journal*. Providence, RI) p. S. 13
[191] Ibid
[192] Ibid
[193] Ibid
[194] Ibid
[195] Ibid
[196] Ibid
[197] Ibid
[198] Breton, Tracy; February 28, 2004: The DiPrete Pension Case – How Needy Is She (*The Providence Journal*. Providence, RI) p. 1
[199] Ibid
[200] Ibid
[201] Ibid

Notes to Chapter 4 – It's Not My Loan: North Providence Acting Finance Director Maria Vallee
[202] The official transcript of the records of the North Providence Town Council, October, 2010.
[203] Ibid
[204] Report on the North Providence Community Development Block Grant Program issued by the United States Office of Housing and Urban Development's Office of Inspector General, 2011.
[205] Ibid
[206] Ibid
[207] Complaint to the United States District Court, Stipulation for Entry of Consent Judgement, filed by the Office of the United States Attorney on July 9, 2013 in the case of US vs. Maria Vallee, C.A.NO.:13-5126.
[208] Rhode Island Ethics Commission Complaint No. 2010-9, Informal Resolution and Settlement.
[209] Ibid
[210] Ibid

[41]Hilario, Mario, North Providence Town Councilor Criticizes Mayor in Wake of Finance Appointment, NBC 10 News, November 23, 2015.

[212] Duane Lockard, New England State Politics (Princeton: Princeton University Press, 1959), p. 178.

[213] Ibid

[214] Patrick T. Conley, Rhode Island in Rhetoric and Reflection: Public Addresses and Essays (Rhode Island Publications Society, 2002), p 407.

[215] Ibid

[216] Lockard, Duane, New England State Politics (Princeton: Princeton University Press, 1959), p. 178.

[217] Conley, Patrick T. Conley, Rhode Island in Rhetoric and Reflection: Public Addresses and Essays (Rhode Island Publications Society, 2002), p 408.

[218] Lockard, Duane, New England State Politics (Princeton: Princeton University Press, 1959), p. 178.

[219] Ibid

[220] Greenstein, Fred I., The Changing Patterns of Urban Party Politics (The Annals, May, 1964) p. 8

[221] Bakst, M. Charles, January 1, 1935: "The Bloodless Revolution" On That Day, Democratic Coup Changed State Government (*The Providence Journal-Bulletin*, October 13, 1985) pg. C-01

[222] Ibid

[223] Ibid

[224] Ibid

[225] Ibid

[226] Ibid

Notes to Chapter 6 – McMansions: The Johnston Zoning Board of Review
[227] Transcript of the Johnston Zoning Board Meeting of May 30, 2013

[228] Ibid

[229] Ibid

[230] Ibid

[231] Ibid

[232] Ibid

[233] Ibid

[234] Ibid

[235] Superior Court Filings for Carol LaCourse v. Bernard Frezza, Anthony Pilozzi, Joseph Anzelone, Richard Fascia, Thomas Lopardo, Dennis Cardillo, Albert Colannino and Joseph Chiodo. C.A. NO: PC13, Complaint, 7/15/13 and Notice of Filing of Appeal, 7/19/13

[236] Ibid

[237] Ibid

[238] Ibid

[239] Superior Court Decision in the Case of Carol Lacourse v. Bernard Frezza, Anthony Pilozzi, Joseph Anzelone, Richard Fascia, Thomas Lopardo, Dennis Cardillo, Albert Colannino and Joseph Chiodo. C.A. No. PC 2013-3469 April 11, 2014.

[240] Testimony of Brian Quirk before the North Providence Town Council, July 2, 2013.
Notes to Chapter 7 - Politicians Protecting Their Own
[241] Ibid

242 North Providence Police Incident Report #06-1317-OF.

243 Ibid

244 North Providence Police Incident Reports #06-1317-OF and #06-1565-OF.

245 North Providence Police Incident Report #06-1880-OF.

246 Testimony of Brian Quirk before the North Providence Town Council, July 2, 2013, and testimony and material presented at the subsequent North Providence Town Council's Ordinance Committee.

247 North Providence Police Incident Report #06-2359-OF

248 Testimony of Brian Quirk before the North Providence Town Council, July 2, 2013, and testimony and material presented at the subsequent North Providence Town Council's Ordinance Committee, and North Providence Police Incident Report #06-2585-OF.

249 North Providence Police Arrest Report #06-1516-AR andTestimony of Brian Quirk before the North Providence Town Council, July 2, 2013, and testimony and material presented at the subsequent North Providence Town Council's Ordinance Committee.

250 Testimony of Brian Quirk before the North Providence Town Council, July 2, 2013, and testimony and material presented at the subsequent North Providence Town Council's Ordinance Committee.

251 Testimony of Brian Quirk before the North Providence Town Council, July 2, 2013, and testimony and material presented at the subsequent North Providence Town Council's Ordinance Committee.

252 Written statement of Frank Manfredi in which he recounts the evening conversation with Giammarco and offers to take a polygraph test, August 10, 2007, submitted as part of the Testimony of Brian Quirk before the North Providence Town Council, July 2, 2013, and testimony and material presented at the subsequent North Providence Town Council's Ordinance Committee.

253 North Providence Police Incident Report #08-1857-OF.

254 North Providence Police incident Reports #07-1838-OF and #08-757-OF

255 Testimony of Brian Quirk before the North Providence Town Council, July 2, 2013, and testimony and material presented at the subsequent North Providence Town Council's Ordinance Committee.

256 RI Superior Court Records – C.A NO.: PC2007-4622.

257 Testimony of Brian Quirk before the North Providence Town Council, July 2, 2013, and testimony and material presented at the subsequent North Providence Town Council's Ordinance Committee.

258 Ibid and North Providence Police Incident Report #08-1265-OF.

259 Ibid.

260 ibid

261 RI Superior Court Records – C.A. NO.: 2008-4817

262 North Providence Zoning Violation Order, November 18, 2008.

263 Testimony of Brian Quirk before the North Providence Town Council, July 2, 2013, and testimony and material presented at the subsequent North Providence Town Council's Ordinance Committee.

264 Ibid

BIBLIOGRAPHY

Books

Conley, Patrick T, Liberty and Justice: A History of Law and Lawyers in Rhode Island, 1936-1998 . (Rhode Island Publications Society, 1998)

Conley, Patrick T, Rhode Island in Rhetoric and Reflection: Public Addresses and Essays (Rhode Island Publications Society, 2002), p 407 & 408.

Horvitz, Leslie Alan, Corruption Reaches Fork In The Rhode – Political Corruption In Rhode Island, (News World Communications, Inc., 1993 The Gale Group, 2004)

Lanza, Steven P. Executive Editor of the Connecticut Economic Quarterly, Winter 2004 Issue, February 24, 2004; (Connecticut Center For Economic Analysis, University of Connecticut)

Lockard, Duane, New England State Politics (Princeton: Princeton University Press, 1959), p. 178.

Periodicals

Bakst, M. Charles, January 1, 1935: "The Bloodless Revolution" On That Day, Democratic Coup Changed State Government (*The Providence Journal-Bulletin*, October 13, 1985) pg. C-01

Breton, Tracy; February 28, 2004: The DiPrete Pension Case – How Needy Is She (*The Providence Journal*. Providence, RI) p. 1

Castellucci, John, Sarault Says He's Changed Man As He Seeks Mass. Law License: October 16, 2001 (*The Providence Journal*, Providence)

Former Mayor Gets 5 ½ Years For Extortion: February 2, 1992 (*The New York Times*, New York)

Freeman, Scott and Malinowski, W. Zachary, August 18, 1991: Behind The Charm, Known For His Fancy Tastes as a Kid, Sarault's Political Ascent Was Unfazed by His Grownup Financial Dealings, Part 1 of 2 parts (*The Providence Journal*, Providence, RI)

Greenstein, Fred I., The Changing Patterns of Urban Party Politics (The Annals, May, 1964) p. 8

Hill, John., November 28, 1999: Public Trust in Police and Politics is Shaken by Scandals (*The Providence Journal*. Providence, RI)

Hill, John, Legal Moves Made In Bribery Case: November 1, 2007 (*The Providence Journal,* Providence)

Hill, John, Oster Treatment Of Picerno Described, January 31, 2008 (*The Providence Journal*, Providence)

Hill, John, Oster Tainted Property In Testimony At Oster Trial, February 1, 2008 (*The Providence Journal*, Providence)

Hill, John, Testimony Centers On $25,000 Payoff: February 6, 2008 (*The Providence Journal*, Providence)

Hill, John, Builder Testifies In Oster Trial: February 7, 2008 (*The Providence Journal*, Providence)

Hill, John, Former Official's Testimony Heard In Oster Bribery Case: February 8, 2008 (*The Providence Journal*, Providence)

Hill, John, Oster Case Could Wrap Up Next Week: February 16, 2008 (*The Providence Journal*, Providence)

Hill, John, Lincoln Official Urged To Resign: February 18, 2002 (*The Providence Journal*, Providence)

Hill, John, Shocker In Lincoln: February 19, 2002 (*The Providence Journal*, Providence)

Hill, John, Jury Set To Decide Oster's Bribery Case: February 20, 2008 (*The Providence Journal*, Providence)

Hill, John, Jury Set To Decide Oster's Bribery Case: February 20, 2008 (*The Providence Journal*, Providence)

Hill, John, Jury Finds Oster Guilty Of Bribery And Extortion Charges: February 22, 2008 (*The Providence Journal*, Providence)

Hill, John, Oster Dead; Apparent Suicide: February 23, 2008 (*The Providence Journal*, Providence)

Hill, John, Counseling Offered To Oster Jury: February 26, 2008 (*The Providence Journal*, Providence)

Malinowski, W. Zachary and Freeman, Scott, October 5, 1991: Grand Jury Indicts Sarault For Third Time. Public Works Director Also Charged. (*The Providence Journal*, Providence, RI)

Mooney, Tom, June 14, 1991: Offer Left Weygand "Speechless" (*The Providence Journal*, Providence, RI)

Rakowsky, Judy, June 13, 1991: Pawtucket's Sarault Faces Extortion, Mail Fraud Charges; Mayor Arrested in His Office by FBI Agents (*The Providence Journal*, Providence, RI)

Stanton, Mike; Breton, Tracy; Herzog, David; Malinowski, Zachary W., August 16, 1998: Rhode Island on Trial – The story of the case against Edward DiPrete, Part two Chapter 15 Teachings - Through Turmoil and Tragedy, the State's Case Moves Ahead (*The Providence Sunday Journal*. Providence, RI) p. S. 01, p. S. 04, p. S. 05, p. S. 08, p. S. 10, p. S. 11, p. S. 13, p. S. 15.

Ziner, Karen Lee, Lincoln Town Administrator Is Charged With Bribery: January 17, 2001 (*The Providence Journal*, Providence)

Hearing Panel Report, S.J.C. Order Denying Reinstatement Entered By Justice Sosman: July 29, 2002

Government Records

Final Report of the Finance Committee of the North Providence Town Council Regarding the Administration of the HUD Loan Program, September 30, 2010.

Johnston Building Records

Johnston Planning Records

Johnston Zoning Records.

North Providence Town Council Records and Meeting Transcripts.

North Providence Police Department Records.

North Providence Zoning Records.

The Office of the United States Attorney, Press Release.

Rhode Island Ethics Commission Complaint No. 2010-9, Internal Resolution and Settlement.

Rhode Island Superior Court Records.

Interviews Conducted by the Author

Interview with Brian Quirk

PHOTO CREDITS

Bob Weygand, from the collection of Paul Caranci, p. 4.
Brian Sarault, courtesy of *The Woonsocket Call*, p. 5.
Pawtucket mayor's door, courtesy of *The Woonsocket Call* p. 6.
Brian Sarault, courtesy of *The Woonsocket Call*, p. 12.
Brian Sarault, courtesy of *The Woonsocket Call*, p. 14.
Brian Sarault, courtesy of *The Woonsocket Call*, p. 17.
Brian Sarault, courtesy of *The Woonsocket Call*, p. 18.
Bob Weygand, from The Rhode Island Manual, C651, Rhode Island Archives, p. 20.
Jonathan Oster, courtesy of *The Woonsocket Call*, p. 22.
The Limerock Center, photo by Thomas Blacke, p. 23.
Lincoln Town Hall, photo by Thomas Blacke, p. 24.
Jonathan Oster, courtesy of *The Woonsocket Call*, p. 35.
RI State House, from the collection of Paul Caranci, p. 44.
Governor Edward DiPrete, The Rhode Island Manual, C651, Rhode Island Archives, p. 57.
Governor Edward DiPrete, The Rhode Island Manual, C651, Rhode Island Archives, p. 74.
Jeff Pine, The Rhode Island Manual, C651, Rhode Island Archives, p. 93.
Attorney General Arlene Violet, The Rhode Island Manual, C651, Rhode Island Archives, p. 110.
North Providence Town Hall, from the collection of Paul Caranci, p. 122.
Lombardi, Vallee, and Fossa, *The Providence Journal,* p. 127.
Vallee home, from the collection of Paul Caranci, p. 129.
Finance committee report, photo by Paul Caranci, p. 133
General Charles Ray Brayton, image and caption reprinted from Rhode Island in Rhetoric and Reflection: Public Addresses and Essays by Patrick T. Conley, p. 138.
Charles Brayton cartoon, *The Providence Journal*, p. 140.
RI State House, from the collection of Paul Caranci, p. 141
Green, McGrath, Truman, Department of Public Works, C1851 Rhode Island State Collection, p. 143.
T.F. Green, 1935 photo from the Rhode Island manual, C651 Rhode Island State Archives, p. 146.
Johnston Town Hall, from the collection of Paul Caranci, p. 154.
Bishop Hill home, photo by Paul Caranci, p. 175.
Brian Quirk, *The North Providence Breeze*, p. 178.
Quirk home, photo provided by Brian Quirk, p. 180.
Giammarco flyer, from the collection of Paul Caranci, p. 181.
Police report, provided by Brian Quirk, p. 182.
Evidence, photo by Paul Caranci, p. 184.
Police statement, provided by Brian Quirk, p. 186.
Lombardi letter, from the collection of Paul Caranci, p. 189.
Giammarco article, *The Providence Journal*, p. 193.

ABOUT THE AUTHORS

Paul F. Caranci is a historian and serves on the board of directors for the RI Heritage Hall of Fame. He is a cofounder of, and consultant to The Municipal Heritage Group and the author of five published books including two produced by The History Press. *North Providence: A History & The People Who Shaped It* (2012) and *The Hanging & Redemption of John Gordon: The True Story of Rhode Island's Last Execution* (2013) that was selected by *The Providence Journal* as one of the top five non-fiction books of 2013. Paul served for eight years as Rhode Island's Deputy Secretary of State and for almost seventeen years as a councilman in his hometown of North Providence. He is married to his high school sweetheart, Margie. They have two adult children, Heather and Matthew, and four grandsons, Matthew Jr., Jacob, Vincent and Casey.

Thomas Blacke has devoted his life to marketing, media and public relations and currently runs his own marketing, PR and security consulting firm. He has worked on many high level political campaigns, served as a lobbyist, and has held leadership positions in the local Democrat Party. Thom is also a professional magician and escape artist who holds multiple Guinness® World Records for escape artistry with ten world records in all. Blacke is the Editor/Publisher of an international magazine and the co-creator of a TV reality show. This is his seventh book.